PENGUIN ANANDA

INNER ENGINEERING

Yogi, mystic, and visionary, Sadhguru is a spiritual master with a difference. Absolute clarity of perception places him in a unique space, not only in matters spiritual but in business, environmental, and international affairs, and opens a new door on all that he touches.

Probing and passionate, insightful, logical, and unfailingly witty, Sadhguru's talks have earned him the reputation of a speaker and opinion-maker of international renown. He has been a lead speaker at the United Nations General Assembly, a regular at the World Economic Forum, and a special invitee at the Australian Leadership Retreat, Indian Economic Summit, and TED. His astute and incisive grasp of world affairs, as well as his unerringly scientific approach to human well-being have had a transformative influence at establishments such as the World Bank, House of Lords (UK), World Presidents' Organization, Massachusetts Institute of Technology, London Business School, Google, and Microsoft, to name a few.

With a celebratory engagement with life on all levels, Sadhguru's areas of active involvement encompass fields as diverse as architecture and visual design, poetry and painting, ecology and horticulture, sports and music. He is the designer of several unique buildings and consecrated spaces at the Isha Yoga Center, which have received wide attention for their combination of intense sacred power with strikingly innovative eco-friendly aesthetics.

Sadhguru is also the founder of Isha Foundation, a non-profit organization dedicated to the well-being of the individual and the world for the past three decades. Isha Foundation does not promote any particular ideology, religion, or race, but transmits inner sciences of universal appeal.

http://isha.sadhguru.org
http://facebook.com/Sadhguru

http://youtube.com/Sadhguru
Twitter: @SadhguruJV

INNER ENGINEERING
✦— A YOGI'S GUIDE TO JOY —✦

SADHGURU

PENGUIN
ANANDA

An imprint of Penguin Random House

PENGUIN ANANDA

USA | Canada | UK | Ireland | Australia
New Zealand | India | South Africa | China

Penguin Ananda is part of the Penguin Random House group of companies
whose addresses can be found at global.penguinrandomhouse.com

Published by Penguin Random House India Pvt. Ltd
7th Floor, Infinity Tower C, DLF Cyber City,
Gurgaon 122 002, Haryana, India

Penguin
Random House
India

First published in the United States by Spiegel & Grau, an imprint of Random
House, a division of Penguin Random House LLC, New York 2016
First published in India in Penguin Ananda by Penguin Random House India 2016

Grateful acknowledgment is made to Penguin UK, a Penguin Random
House Company, for permission to reprint an excerpt from *Speaking of Siva*,
translated with an introduction by A. K. Ramanujan (Penguin Classics, 1973).
Copyright © 1973 by A. K. Ramanujan. Reprinted by permission.

The views and opinions expressed in this book are the author's own and the
facts are as reported by him which have been verified to the extent possible,
and the publishers are not in any way liable for the same. Some names and
identifying details have been changed.

ISBN 9780143428848

For sale in the Indian Subcontinent only

Book design by Dana Leigh Blanchette
Printed at Thomson Press India Ltd, New Delhi

www.penguin.co.in

Contents

INNER ENGINEERING

The Four-Letter Word

Once it happened . . . A customer walking into Shankaran Pillai's pharmacy saw a man outside hugging a lamppost, his eyeballs rolling wildly.

When he walked in, he asked, "Who's that man? What's wrong with him?"

Shankaran Pillai replied, unperturbed, "Oh, that guy. He's one of my customers."

"But what's the matter with him?"

"He wanted something for a whooping cough. I gave him the appropriate medicine."

"What did you give him?"

"A box of laxatives. I made him take it right here."

"Laxatives for a whooping cough! Why on earth would you give him that?"

"Oh come on, you saw him. You think he dares to cough anymore?"

Shankaran Pillai's box of laxatives is emblematic of the type of solution being peddled all over the world today for those in search of well-being. It is the fundamental reason the term "guru" has become a four-letter word.

Unfortunately, we have forgotten the real meaning of the word. "Guru" literally means "dispeller of darkness." The function of the guru, contrary to popular belief, is not to teach, indoctrinate, or convert. The guru is here to throw light on dimensions beyond your sensory perceptions and your psychological drama, dimensions that you are currently unable to perceive. The guru is here, fundamentally, to throw light on the very nature of your existence.

There are many spurious and dangerously misleading teachings in vogue in our world today. "Be in the moment" is one of them. The assumption is that you could be somewhere else, if you wanted. How is that even possible? The present is the only place that you *can* be. If you live, you live in *this* moment. If you die, you die in *this* moment. This moment is eternity. How are you going to escape it, even if you try?

Right now your problem is that you suffer what happened ten years ago and you suffer what may happen the day after tomorrow. Both are not living truths. They are simply a play of your memory and imagination. Does this mean then that in order to find peace you must annihilate your mind? Not at all. It simply means you need to take charge of it. Your mind carries the enormous reserves of memory and the incredible possibilities of the imagination that are the result of an evolutionary process of millions of years. If you can use it when you want and put it aside when you don't, the mind can be a fantastic tool. To shun the past and neglect the future is to trivialize this wonderful faculty. So "be in the moment" becomes a crippling psychological restriction—it denies our existential reality.

"Do only one thing at a time" has become another popular self-help slogan. Why would you do only one thing when the mind is a phenomenal multidimensional machine, capable of handling several levels of activity all at once? Instead of harnessing and learning to ride the mind, why would you want to obliterate it? When you can know the heady joy of mental action, why would you opt for a lobotomy, for voluntary cabbage-hood?

The other phrase that has hardened into cliché through overuse is "positive thinking." When it is oversimplified and used as some quick-fix mantra, positive thinking becomes a way of whitewashing or sugarcoating your reality. When you are unable to process real-time information and control your psychological drama, you seize on "positive thinking" as a tranquilizer. Initially, it might seem to imbue your life with new confidence and optimism. But it is essentially limited. In the long term, if you deny or amputate one part of reality, it gives you a lopsided perspective of life.

Then there is the time-honored business of exporting human well-being to the heavens and claiming that the core of the universe is love. Love is a *human* possibility. If you need a refresher course, you can take lessons from your dog. He is full of love! You don't have to go to outer space to know love. All these puerile philosophies come from the assumption that existence is human-centric. This single idea has robbed us of all sense and made us commit some of the most inhuman and heinous crimes throughout history. These continue to perpetuate themselves to this very day.

As a guru, I have no doctrine to teach, no philosophy to impart, no belief to propagate. And that is because the only solution for all the ills that plague humanity is self-transformation. Self-transformation is not incremental self-improvement. Self-transformation is achieved not by morals or ethics or attitudinal or behavioral changes, but by experiencing the limitless nature of who we are. Self-transformation means nothing of the old remains. It is a dimensional shift in the way you perceive and experience life.

Knowing this is yoga. One who embodies this is a yogi. One who guides you in this direction is a guru.

My aim in this book is to help make joy your constant companion. To make that happen, this book offers you not a sermon, but a science; not a teaching, but a technology; not a precept, but a path. It is now time to start exploring that science, working the technology, walking the path.

On this journey, the guru is not the destination but the road map. The inner dimension is uncharted terrain. If you are exploring terrain that is unfamiliar to you, isn't it better to have signposts? You could find your own way, but who knows, it could take lifetimes. When you're on unfamiliar terrain, it's just sensible to take directions. On one level, that is all a guru is—a live road map. GPS: Guru Pathfinding System!

And *that's* why there exists that infamous four-letter word.

Just to make things doubly easy for you, I thought I'd make it eight . . .

. . . Sadhguru

PART ONE

A Note to the Reader

There are many ways to approach a book of this kind. One way would be to plunge directly into practice, to take a headlong dive into do-it-yourself mode. But then this book doesn't claim to be a self-help manual. It has a strong practical orientation, but there's more to it than that.

Another way would be to turn theoretical. But this book is not an exercise in scholarship either. I have never read any of the yogic treatises in their entirety. I never had to. I come from inner experience. It was only late in my life when I skimmed through some of Patanjali's *Yoga Sutras,* those significant yogic texts, that I realized that I had a certain access to their inner core. This is because I approach them experientially, rather than theoretically. To reduce a sophisticated science, like yoga, to mere doctrine is just as tragic as turning it into a cardiovascular workout.

And so, this book has finally been divided into two sections. The first maps the terrain; the second offers you a way to navigate it.

What you are about to read in this section is not a display

of academic expertise. Instead, this section seeks to offer a series of fundamental insights—insights that lay the foundation or bedrock on which the architecture of the more practice-oriented second section is built.

These insights are not tenets or teachings. And they are most definitely not conclusions. They are best seen as signposts on a journey that can be made by no one but you. They are core perspectives that have emerged as a consequence of the state of heightened awareness that has been mine since a life-transforming experience thirty-three years ago.

The section begins on an autobiographical note. This is so you know something about the authorial company you will be keeping, should you choose to read the rest of the book! The section then unfolds into an examination of certain basic ideas, exploring along the way some commonly used (and misused) terms such as destiny, responsibility, well-being, and even more fundamentally, yoga.

One of the chapters in this section closes with a *sadhana*. The word "sadhana" in Sanskrit means a device or a tool. These tools for exploration offer a chance for you as a reader to put the ideas discussed in those pages into action and see if the insights work for you. (These sadhanas will recur much more frequently in Section Two.)

I am often told by people that I seem to be a "modern" guru. My response to that observation is that I am neither modern nor ancient, neither new age nor old age. I am contemporary, and that is how every guru has always been. Only scholars, pundits, and theologians are capable of being ancient or modern. A philosophy or belief system can be old or new. But gurus are always contemporary.

A guru, as I said earlier, is someone who dispels darkness, someone who opens the door for you. If I promise to open a door for you tomorrow or I opened it for someone else yesterday, it is of no relevance. Only if I open a door for you today is it of some value.

So, the truth is timeless, but the technology and the language are *always* contemporary. If they weren't, they would deserve to be discarded. No tradition, however time-honored, deserves to live on as anything more than a museum piece if it has outlived its relevance. So, while I will be exploring an ancient technology in this book, it is also a technology that is flawlessly state-of-the-art.

Personally, I am not interested in offering anything new. I am only interested in what is true. But I hope that the following section will offer you some moments when the two converge. For at those junctures when the conditions are right—when an insight is articulated from a place of inner clarity and when it meets a reader at the right moment of receptivity, an age-old truth turns explosively alchemical. All of a sudden, it is fresh, alive, radiantly new, as if uttered and heard for the very first time in history.

When I Lost My Sense

> Then I was a man
> I only went up the Hill
> As I had time to kill
> But kill I did all that was
> Me and Mine
>
> With Me and Mine gone
> Lost all my will and skill
> Here I am, an empty vessel
> Enslaved to the Divine Will
> and infinite skill

In the city of Mysore, there is a tradition. If you have something to do, you go up Chamundi Hill. And if you have nothing to do, you go up Chamundi Hill. If you fall in love, you go up Chamundi Hill. And if you fall out of love, you *have* to go up Chamundi Hill.

One afternoon, I had nothing to do, and I had recently fallen out of love, so I went up Chamundi Hill.

I parked my motorcycle and sat on an outcrop of rock about two-thirds of the way uphill. This was my "contemplation rock." It had been for some time now. A purple berry tree and a stunted banyan had put down tenacious roots into a deep fissure in the rock surface. A panoramic view of the city unfolded before me.

Until that moment, in my experience, my body and mind was "me" and the world was "out there." But suddenly I did not know what was me and what was not me. My eyes were still open. But the air that I was breathing, the rock on which I was sitting, the very atmosphere around, everything had become me. I was everything that was. I was conscious, but I had lost my senses. The discriminatory nature of the senses simply did not exist anymore. The more I say, the crazier it will sound because what was happening was indescribable. What was me was literally *everywhere*. Everything was exploding beyond defined boundaries; everything was exploding into everything else. It was a dimensionless unity of absolute perfection.

My life is just that moment, gracefully enduring.

When I returned to my normal senses, it felt as if just ten minutes had elapsed. But a glance at my watch told me that it was seven thirty in the evening! Four and a half hours had passed. My eyes were open, the sun had set, and it was dark. I was fully aware, but what I had considered to be myself until that moment had completely disappeared.

I have never been the teary kind. And yet, here I was, at the age of twenty-five, on a rock on Chamundi Hill, so ecstatically crazy that the tears were flowing and my entire shirt was wet!

Being peaceful and happy had never been an issue for me. I had lived my life the way I wanted. I had grown up in the sixties, the era of the Beatles and blue jeans, read my share of European philosophy and literature—Dostoyevsky, Camus, Kafka, and the like. But here I was exploding into a completely different dimension of existence of which I knew nothing, drenched in a completely new feeling—an exuberance, a blissfulness—that I had never known or imagined possible. When I applied my skeptical mind to this, the only thing my mind could tell me was that maybe I was going off my rocker! Still, it was so beautiful that I knew that I didn't want to lose it.

I have never quite been able to describe what happened that afternoon. Perhaps the best way to put it is that I went up and didn't come down. I never have.

I was born in Mysore, a pretty princely town in southern India, an erstwhile capital, known for its palaces and gardens. My father was a physician, my mother a homemaker. I was the youngest of four siblings.

School bored me. I found sitting through class impossible because I could see that the teachers were talking about something that did not mean anything to their lives. Every day, as a four-year-old, I instructed my housekeeper, who accompanied me to school in the morning, to drop me off at the gates and not enter the building. As soon as she left, I would dart to the nearby canyon, which exploded with an incredible variety of life. I started accumulating a vast personal zoo of insects, tadpoles, and snakes in bottles obtained from my father's medicine cabinet. After a few months, when my parents discovered that I hadn't been attending school, however, they seemed singularly unimpressed by my biological explorations. My expeditions to the canyon were dismissed as messing about in a rainwater drain. Thwarted, as I often was, by what I regarded as a dull and unimaginative adult world, I simply turned my attention elsewhere and found something else to do.

In later years, I preferred to spend my days roaming the forest, catching snakes, fishing, trekking, and climbing trees. I would often climb to the topmost branch of a big tree, with my lunch box and water bottle. The swaying motion of the branches would transport me to a trancelike state, where I was asleep but wide awake at the same time. I would lose all sense of time on this tree. I would be perched there from nine o'clock in the morning to four thirty in the evening when the bell rang and school was done. Much later, I realized that unknowingly I was becoming meditative at this stage in my life. Later, when I first instructed people into meditations, it was always swaying meditations. Of course, I hadn't even heard of the word "meditation" at this point. I simply liked the way the tree swayed me into a state beyond sleep and wakefulness.

I found the classroom dull but I was interested in everything else—the way the world is made, the physical terrain of the land, the way people live. I used to take my bicycle along the mud roads in the countryside, riding a minimum of thirty-five kilometers a day. By the time I came home, I'd be caked with layers of mud and dust. I particularly enjoyed making mental maps of the terrain I'd traveled. I could just close my eyes when I was alone and re-draw the entire landscape that

I'd seen that afternoon—every single rock, every outcrop, every single tree. I was fascinated by the different seasons, the way the land changes when it is ploughed, when the crops start germinating. That is what drew me to the work of Thomas Hardy: his descriptions of the English landscape which go on for pages on end. I was doing the same in my head with the world around me. Even today it is like a video in my head. If I want I can replay the whole thing, those years and years of all that I observed, with vivid clarity.

I was a diehard skeptic. Even at the age of five, when my family went to the temple, I had questions—lots of them. Who is God? Where is He? Up there? Where is up? A couple of years later, I had even more questions. In school, they said the planet was round. But if the planet was round, how did one know which way was up? No one ever managed to answer these questions, so I never entered the temple. This meant they were compelled to leave me in the custody of the footwear attendant outside. The attendant held me by the arm in a viselike grip, pulling and tugging me around with him as he did his business. He knew that if he looked the other way I'd be gone! Later in my life, I couldn't help noticing that people coming out of restaurants always had more joyful faces than those coming out of temples. That intrigued me.

And yet, while I was a skeptic, I never identified with that label either. I had lots of questions about everything, but never felt the need to draw any conclusions. I realized very early that I knew nothing about anything. That meant I ended up paying enormous attention to everything around me. If someone gave me a glass of water, I stared at it endlessly. If I picked up a leaf, I stared at it endlessly too. I stared at the darkness all night. If I looked at a pebble, the image would rotate interminably in my mind, so I would know its every grain, its every angle.

I also saw that language was no more than a conspiracy devised by human beings. If someone spoke, I realized they were only making sounds, and I was making up the meanings. So, I stopped making up meanings and the sounds became very amusing. I could see patterns spewing out of their mouths. If I kept staring, the person would just disintegrate and turn into a blob of energy. Then all that was left was patterns!

In this state of absolute borderless ignorance, just about anything could hold my attention. My dear father, being a physician, began to think I needed psychiatric evaluation. In his words, "This boy is staring unblinkingly at something all the time. He's lost it!" It has always seemed to me odd that the world does not realize the immensity of a state of "I do not know." Those who destroy that state with beliefs and assumptions completely miss an enormous possibility—the possibility of knowing. They forget that "I do not know" is the doorway—the *only* doorway—to seeking and knowing.

My mother instructed me to pay attention to my teachers. And I did. I paid them the kind of attention they would never have received anywhere else! I had no idea what they were saying, but on those occasions when I attended class, I stared at them, unwavering and intense. For some reason, they did not find this trait particularly endearing. One particular teacher did everything possible to elicit a response from me. But when I remained silent and taciturn, he seized me by the shoulder and shook me violently. "Either you're the divine or the devil," he declared. He added, "And I think you're the latter!"

I was not particularly insulted. Until that moment, I had approached everything around me—from a grain of sand to the universe—with a sense of wonder. But there had always been one certainty in this complex web of questions and that was "me." But my teacher's outburst triggered another line of inquiry. Who was I? Human, divine, devil, what? I tried to stare at myself to find out. It didn't work. So, I closed my eyes and tried to find out. Minutes turned to hours, and I continued to sit, eyes closed.

When my eyes were open, everything intrigued me—an ant, a leaf, clouds, flowers, darkness, just about anything. But to my amazement, I found that with my eyes closed, there was even more that grabbed my attention—the way the body pulses, the way different organs function, the various channels along which one's inner energy moves, the manner in which the anatomy is aligned, the fact that boundaries are limited to the external world. This exercise opened up the entire mechanics of being human before me. Instead of leading me to a simplistic answer that I was "this" or "that," it gradually brought me to a realization that, if I were willing, I could be everything. It wasn't about arriving at any conclusions. Even the certainty of "me" collapsed as a deeper sense of what it is to be a human being started opening up. From knowing myself as an autonomous person, this exercise melted me down. I became a nebulous being.

Despite all my wild ways, the one thing I did manage to do in a strangely disciplined fashion was my practice of yoga. It started one summer vacation when I was twelve. A whole bunch of us cousins met every year in my grandfather's ancestral home. In the backyard there stood an old well, over 150 feet deep. While the girls played hide-and-seek, the regular game played by us boys was to jump into the well and then climb up again. Both jumping down and climbing up were a challenge. If you didn't do it properly, your brains could become a smear on the wall. While you were climbing up, there were no steps; you simply had to clutch at the rock surface and claw yourself up. Your fingernails often bled out of sheer pressure. Just a few of the boys could do this. I was one of them and I was pretty good at it.

One day a man of over seventy years of age appeared. He watched us for a while. Without a word, he jumped into the well. We thought he was finished. But he climbed out quicker than me. I cast aside my pride and asked him just one question: How? "Come, learn yoga," said the old man.

I followed him like a puppy. And that's how I became a student of Malladihalli Swami (as this old man was known) and got into yoga. In the past, waking me up every morning was a family project. My family would try to make me sit up in bed; I would keel over and fall asleep again. My mother would hand me my toothbrush; I would stick it into my mouth and fall asleep. In desperation, she would push me into the bathroom; I would promptly fall asleep again. But three months after starting yoga, my body started coming awake at three forty every morning, without any external prompting, as it does even today. After I woke, my practices would simply happen, no matter where I was and in what situation, without a single day's break. This simple yoga—called *angamardana* (a system of physical yoga that strengthens sinews and limbs)—definitely set me apart in any group of people, physically and mentally. But that's about all. Or so I believed.

In time, I lost all faith in structured education. It wasn't cynicism. I had enough zest and life in me to keep me involved in everything. But my dominant quality even at this age was clarity. I was not actively looking for inconsistencies or loopholes in anything I was taught. I just saw them. I have never looked for anything in my life. I just look. And that is what I am trying to teach people now: if you really want to know spirituality, don't look *for* anything. People think spirituality is about looking for God or truth or the ultimate. The problem is you have already defined what you are looking for. It is not the object of your search that is important; it is the faculty of looking. The ability to simply look without motive is missing in the world today. Everybody is a psychological creature, wanting to assign meaning to everything. Seeking is not about looking for something. It is about enhancing your perception, your very faculty of seeing.

After high school, I embarked on a self-study program at the Mysore University Library. I was the first person there in the morning at nine and the last to be shooed out at eight thirty at night. Between breakfast and dinner, my only sustenance was books. Although I was always ravenous, I skipped lunch for a whole year. I read widely, from Homer to *Popular Mechanics*, Kafka to Kalidasa, Dante to Dennis the Menace. I emerged from that one year more knowledgeable, but with more questions than ever before.

My mother's tears compelled me to enroll grudgingly in Mysore University as a student of English literature. But I continued to carry the cloud of a billion questions, like a dark halo around me, all the time. Neither the library nor my professors could dispel it. Once again I spent most of my time outside the classroom rather than in it. I found that all that was happening in class was the dictation of notes, and I was definitely not planning to be a stenographer! I once asked a lecturer to give me her notes so I could photocopy them; it would save her the trouble of dictation and me the trouble of attending. Finally, I made a deal with all the teachers (who were more than happy not to have me in class). On each day of the month, they would mark me present in class. On the last day of the month the attendance was registered. That day I would enter and just make sure they were keeping up their end of the bargain!

A group of us started meeting under a huge banyan tree on the campus grounds. Someone named it the Banyan Tree Club and the label stuck. The club had a motto: "We do it for the fun of it." We would assemble under the tree on our motorcycles, and talk for hours on a variety of subjects—from how to make Jawa motorcycles go faster than they did to how to make the world a better place. Of course, we would never get off our motorcycles at any point. That would have been sacrilege!

By the time I was done with university, I had ridden all over the country. Initially, I traveled South India on my bicycle. Later I crisscrossed the entire country on my motorcycle. Then it was natural to cross the national borders. But when I reached the India-Nepal frontier, I was told that my motorcycle registration and driving license weren't enough. I needed more papers. After that, it became my dream to somehow earn enough money to travel the world on my motorcycle. It wasn't just wanderlust. The truth is I was restless. I wanted to *know* something. I didn't know what and I didn't know where I needed to go to get it. But in my innermost being, I knew I wanted more.

I never considered myself particularly impulsive; I was just life-oriented. I measured the consequences of my actions; it is just that the more dangerous they were, the more they attracted me. Someone once told me my guardian angel must be very good and perpetually working overtime! There was always in me a longing to test the border, to cross the edge. *What* and *why* were never questions for me. *How* was the only question. When I look back now, I realize that I never thought about what I wanted to become in life. I only thought about how I wanted to live my life. And I knew that the "how" could only be determined within me and by me.

There was a big boom in poultry farming at the time. I wanted to make some money to finance my desire for unrestrained, purposeless travel. So I got into it. My father said, "What am I going to tell people? That my son is rearing chickens?" But I built my poultry farm and I built it single-handedly, from scratch. The business took off. The profits started rolling in. I devoted four hours every morning to the business. The rest of the day was spent reading and writing poetry, swimming in the well, meditating, daydreaming on a huge banyan tree.

Success made me adventurous. My father was always lamenting that everyone else's sons had become engineers, industrialists, joined the civil service, or gone to America. And everywhere everyone I met—my friends, relatives, my old school and college teachers—said, "Oh, we thought you'd make something of your life, but you are just wasting it."

I took on the challenge. In partnership with a civil engineer friend, I entered the construction business. In five years, we became a major construction company, among the leading private contractors in Mysore. My father was incredulous and delighted.

I was exuberant and sure-footed, adrenaline-charged and itching for a challenge. When everything you do is a success, you tend to start believing that the planets revolve around you, not the sun!

And that was the kind of young man I was that fateful afternoon of September 1982 when I decided to get on my Czech motorcycle and ride up Chamundi Hill.

I had no clue then that my life would never be the same again.

Later, when I tried to talk to my friends about what had happened that day up on the mountain, all they could ask was, "Did you drink something? Did you pop something?" They were even more clueless than I was of this new dimension that had suddenly exploded into my life.

Even before I had begun to process what it meant, the experience returned. It was a week later. I was sitting at the dinner table with my family. I thought it lasted two minutes but it was seven hours. I was sitting right there, fully aware, except that the "me" I knew as myself was not there anymore; everything else was. And time flipped.

I remember various members of my family tapping me on the shoulder, asking me what happened, urging me to eat my meal. I simply raised my hand and asked them to leave. They were accustomed to my strange ways by then. They left me alone. It was almost four fifteen in the morning when I returned to my "normal" senses.

The experience began to happen more frequently. When it occurred, I neither ate nor slept for hours on end. I simply sat rooted to a single spot. On one occasion, the experience lasted for up to thirteen days. I happened to be in a village when it began—this state of overwhelming and indescribable stillness and ecstasy. The villagers gathered around me and started whispering to each other, "Oh, he must be in *samadhi*" (a blissful state of being beyond the body, well-documented in Indian spiritual traditions). India, being the country it is, there was a traditional understanding of spirituality to which they were heir that I, with my blue denim–wrapped brain, had no clue about. When I emerged from that state, someone wanted to put a garland around me. Another wanted to touch my feet. It was crazy; I could not believe anyone would want to do this to me.

On another day, I was having lunch. I put a morsel of food in my mouth, and suddenly, it exploded. At that moment, I was able to experience the miraculous alchemy of human digestion—the process by which an external substance, a piece of the planet, was becoming a part of me. We all know this intellectually—that a part of the planet nourishes us, and our bodies, in turn, one day return to nourish the very same earth that once sustained us. But when the knowledge dawned experientially, it altered my fundamental perspective of who I was. My relationship with everything around me, including the planet, went through a dimensional shift.

I grew aware of that extraordinary intelligence within each of us that is capable of transforming a piece of bread or an apple into the human body in a single afternoon. Not a small feat! As I began consciously touching that intelligence, which is the source of creation, seemingly inexplicable events started occurring around me. Things that I touched were transformed in some way or the other. People would look at me and burst into tears. Many claimed that they were relieved of conditions of physical and mental suffering just by looking at me. I found myself healed in a matter of hours of conditions that would have taken me months to get out of through normal medical care. However, I gave all of this little importance.

This ability to transform my external and internal reality quite dramatically has continued within me and around me to this very day. It is not something I have ever tried consciously to achieve. It is just that once one is in touch with this deeper dimension of intelligence, which is the very basis of our existence here, life turns quite naturally miraculous.

In about six to eight weeks, this incredible experience became a living reality. During this time, everything about me changed dramatically. My physical appearance—the shape of my eyes, my gait, my voice, the very alignment of my body— began changing so drastically that people around me started to notice as well.

What was happening inside me was even more phenomenal. Within six weeks, a huge flood of memory descended— literally, lifetimes of memory. I was now aware of a million different things happening inside me in a single moment. It was like a kaleidoscope. My logical mind told me none of this could be true. What I was seeing inside myself was clearer than daylight. But I secretly hoped it was false. I had always seen myself as a smart young man. Suddenly I appeared to be a clueless young fool, and that bewilderment was something I could not come to terms with. But I found to my chagrin that everything my memory was telling me was true.

Until this time, I had completely refused to accept anything in my life that did not fit into a rational and logical framework. Slowly, I began to realize that it is life that is the ultimate intelligence. Human intellect is mere smartness that ensures survival. But true intelligence is just life and life—and that which is the source of life. Nothing else.

The world has been told that the divine is love, that the divine is compassion. But if you pay attention to creation, you realize that the divine, or whatever is the source of creation, is, above all, the highest intelligence that you can imagine. Instead of trying to tap into this all-powerful intelligence that pulsates within each of us, we opt to use our logical intellect, which is useful in certain situations, but essentially limited.

I also began to experience a heightened sensitivity to the feelings of others. Sometimes just the sight of an unknown person on the street in a state of grief could make me weep. I could not believe the states of misery that human beings were capable of enduring when here I was, simply bursting with ecstasy for no reason at all.

It took a while for me to realize that what was happening to me was something "spiritual." I began to understand that what the sacred traditions and scriptures had extolled as the ultimate experience was happening to me; that I was experiencing, in fact, the most beautiful thing that can happen to a human being.

Moment to moment every cell in my body was exploding with nameless ecstasies. Right now people glorify childhood because a child can laugh and be happy for no reason at all. But I saw that it is possible to be ecstatic in one's adulthood as well. It is possible for every human being because all we can ever experience happens from *within* us.

I began to realize that the physical transformation in my appearance was actually a realignment of my entire inner constitution. I had been practicing a basic set of physical postures, or *hatha yoga,* since I was twelve years old. Those thirteen-odd years of yoga bore fruit at this time. Yoga is essentially a way of re-creating the body so that it serves a higher purpose. The human body can function as a piece of flesh and blood or as the very source of creation.

There is a whole technology for transforming the human into the divine. The human spine isn't just a bad arrangement of bones; it is the very axis of the universe. It just depends on how you reorganize your system. In my case, from being a physically intense person, I learnt to carry my body as if it were not there at all. My physicality became very relaxed. Earlier, all that intensity was in my body. People could feel that if I entered a room, it meant action. But now I learned to carry my body differently.

And that is when I realized that this experience I had had was really yoga. This experience of union with existence, of oneness with all life, of boundlessness was yoga. The simple set of yogic postures, or *asanas,* I'd been practicing daily was about physical fitness, or so I thought. But after that experience on Chamundi Hill, I realized that what I was doing was actually a process that could deliver me to a dimension far beyond the physical. And that is why I tell people: even if you get into yoga for the wrong reasons, it still works!

There is something within every human being that dislikes boundaries, that is longing to become boundless. Human nature is such that we always yearn to be something more than what we are right now. No matter how much we achieve, we still want to be something more. If we just looked at this closely, we would realize that this longing is not for more; this longing is for *all*. We are all seeking to become infinite. The only problem is that we are seeking it in installments.

Imagine that you were locked up in a cubicle of five feet by five feet. However comfortable it is, you would long to be free of it. The next day, if you were released into a larger cubicle of ten feet by ten feet, you would feel great for a while, but soon the same longing to break that boundary would return. It does not matter how large a boundary we set, the moment you become conscious of it, the longing to break it is instinctive. In the East, this longing has been culturally recognized as the highest goal of all human activity and endeavor. Freedom—or *mukti* or *moksha*—is seen as the natural longing in every human being and our ultimate destination. It is just because we are unconscious of it that we seek to fulfill it in installments, whether through the acquisition of power, money, love, or knowledge. Or through that other great pastime of today—shopping!

The moment I realized that human desire was not for any particular thing, but just to expand illimitably, a certain clarity rose within me. When I saw that everyone is capable of this, it felt natural to want to share it. My whole aim since then has been to somehow rub this experience off on other people, to awaken them to the fact that this state of joy, of freedom, of limitlessness cannot be denied to them unless they stand in the way of the natural effervescence of life.

This condition of ecstatic well-being that has been mine since that afternoon on Chamundi Hill is neither a distant possibility nor a pipe dream. It is a living reality for those who are willing. It is the birthright of every human being.

The Way Out Is In

Everything you have done in your life so far has been in pursuit of a single thing. Whether you sought a career, started a business, made money, or built a family, it was always because you wanted just one simple thing: joy.

But somewhere along the way, life got complicated.

If you had been born as any other creature on this planet, it would have been very simple. Your needs would have just been physical. A full stomach would have been equivalent to a great day. Take a look at your dog or your cat: the moment their stomach is full, they are quite peaceful.

But when you come into this world as a human being, things change. An empty stomach is one problem: hunger. But a full stomach? A hundred problems! When our survival is in question, it is a big issue in our lives. But the moment it is taken care of, it doesn't seem to mean anything. Somehow, for a human being, life doesn't seem to end with survival; life *begins* with survival.

Today, as a generation of people, our survival process is better organized than ever before. You can go to a supermarket and buy everything you need for the entire year. You can do it without even stepping out of your home! Never before in the history of humanity has such a thing been possible. Things that even royalty could not afford a hundred years ago are accessible to the average citizen. We are the most comfortable generation to have ever lived on this planet. The rub is that we are definitely not the most joyful, or the most loving, or the most peaceful.

Why is this so? We have tried our best to fix the outside environment. If we fix it any more, there will be no planet left! But we are still no happier than our ancestors a thousand years ago. If it is not working, isn't it time to look at what's wrong? How can we continue to do something that has not worked for a thousand years? How much longer are we going to live with blueprints that clearly haven't delivered their promise?

It is time for a paradigm shift.

∞

Let us start with a single question: what do we consider to be a state of well-being?

Very simply, well-being is just a deep sense of *pleasantness* within. If your body feels pleasant, we call this health. If it becomes very pleasant, we call this pleasure. If your mind becomes pleasant, we call this peace. If it becomes very pleasant, we call this joy. If your emotions become pleasant, we call this love. If they become very pleasant, we call this compassion. If your life energies become pleasant, we call this bliss. If they become very pleasant, we call this ecstasy. This is all that you are seeking: pleasantness within and without. When pleasantness is within, it is termed peace, joy, happiness. When your surroundings become pleasant, it gets branded success. If you're not interested in any of this and want to go to heaven, what are you seeking? Just otherworldly success! So, essentially all human experience is only a question of pleasantness and unpleasantness in varying degrees.

But how many times in your life have you lived an entire day blissfully—without a single moment of anxiety, agitation, irritation, or stress? How many times have you lived in utter and absolute pleasantness for twenty-four hours? When was the last time it happened to you?

The amazing thing is that for most people on this planet, not a *single* day has happened exactly the way they want it! Of course, there is no one who has not experienced joy, peace, even bliss, but it is always fleeting. They are unable to sustain it. They manage to get there, but it keeps collapsing. And nothing earth-shattering needs to happen for it to collapse. The simplest things throw people off balance, out of kilter.

It is like this. You go out today and someone tells you that you are the most beautiful person in the world: you're floating on cloud nine. But then you come home, and the folks at home tell you who you *really* are: everything crashes!

Sound familiar?

Why do you need to be pleasant within? The answer is self-evident. When you are in a pleasant inner state, you are naturally pleasant to everyone and everything around you. No scripture or philosophy is needed to instruct you to be good to others. It is a natural outcome when you are feeling good within yourself. Inner pleasantness is a surefire insurance for the making of a peaceful society and a joyful world.

Besides, your success in the world depends essentially on how well you harness the prowess of the body and mind. So, in order to achieve success, pleasantness has to be the fundamental quality within you.

Above all, there is substantial medical and scientific evidence today that your body and mind function at their best when you are in a pleasant state. It is said that if you can remain blissful for twenty-four hours, your intellectual capabilities can be almost doubled. Just settling the internal muddle and allowing clarity to surface can achieve this.

Now, the same life energy that you refer to as "myself" has sometimes been very happy, sometimes miserable, sometimes peaceful, sometimes in turmoil. The same life energy is capable of all those states. So, if you were given a choice about the kind of expression your life energies should find, what would you choose? Joy or misery? Pleasantness or unpleasantness?

The answer is self-evident. The ways may vary from person to person. But whether you're trying to make money, hitting the bottle, or attempting to get to heaven, pleasantness is the only goal. Even if you say you are not interested in this world and your mission in life is only to get to heaven, you're still only searching for pleasantness. If people had told you since your childhood that God lives in heaven, but heaven is a horrendous place, would you want to go there? Definitely not! Essentially, the highest level of pleasantness is heaven; unpleasantness is hell. So, some think it's in the wine, and others think it's in the divine, but pleasantness is what everyone's seeking.

The only thing that stands between you and your well-being is a simple fact: you have allowed your thoughts and emotions to take instruction from the outside rather than the inside.

On a certain day, a lady went to sleep. In her sleep, she had a dream. She saw a hunk of a man, staring at her. Then he started coming closer—closer and closer.

He was so close that she could even feel his breath.

She trembled—not in fear.

Then she asked, "What will you do to me?"

The man said, "Well, lady, it's *your* dream!"

What's happening in your head is *your* dream. At least your dream should happen the way you want it, shouldn't it? Even if the world doesn't happen the way you want it, at least your thoughts and emotions should happen the way you want them to. Right now, these aren't taking instructions from you because you are handling the whole human mechanism accidentally.

The human mechanism is the most sophisticated physical form on the planet. You are the greatest piece of technology, but the problem is you don't know where the keyboard is. It's like you're handling a supercomputer with a pickaxe and a wrench! As a result, the simple life process is taking a toll upon humanity. Just to earn a living, to reproduce, to raise a family, and then one day to fall dead—what a challenge! It is amazing how human beings struggle just to do what every worm, insect, bird, and animal does quite effortlessly.

Put simply, our inner ecology is a mess. Somehow we think that fixing outer conditions will make everything okay on the inside. But these past 150 years are proof that technology will only bring comfort and convenience to us, not well-being. We need to understand that *unless we do the right things, the right things will not happen to us:* this is true not just of the outside world, but also the inside.

∞

On a certain day, a bull and a pheasant were grazing on a field. The bull was grazing and the pheasant was picking ticks off the bull—a perfect partnership. Looking at the huge tree at the edge of the field, the pheasant said, "Alas, there was a time I could fly to the topmost branch of the tree. Now I do not have enough strength in my wing to even get to the first branch."

The bull said nonchalantly, "Just eat a little bit of my dung every day, and watch what happens. Within two weeks, you'll get to the top."

The pheasant said, "Oh come on, that's rubbish. What kind of nonsense is that?"

The bull said, "Try it and see. The whole of humanity is onto it."

Very hesitantly, the pheasant started pecking. And lo, on the very first day, he reached the first branch. Within a fort-night, he had reached the topmost branch. He sat there, just beginning to enjoy the scenery.

The old farmer, rocking on his rocking chair, saw a fat old pheasant on top of the tree. He pulled out his shotgun and shot the bird off the tree.

Moral of the story: bullshit may get you to the top, but it never lets you stay there!

So, you can bullshit yourself into all kinds of emotional states, you can somehow crank up some well-being for yourself, but the problem is, it doesn't last. The weather could bring it down. The stock market could make it come crashing down. And even if it does not collapse, living in anticipation that it might is bad enough! The impending possibility that it will fall apart one day is torture—often worse than the actual disaster. So, as long as your inner life is enslaved to external situations, it will remain a precarious condition. There is no other way for it to be.

What then is the way out?

The way out is a very simple change in direction. You just need to see that the source and basis of your experience is *within* you. Human experience may be stimulated or catalyzed by external situations, but the source is within. Pain or pleasure, joy or misery, agony or ecstasy, happens only inside you. Human folly is that people are always trying to extract joy from the outside. You may use the outside as a stimulus or trigger, but the real thing always comes from within.

Right now, you are holding a book. Where do you see the book? Use your finger and point to where you see it. Do you think the image is outside you?

Think again.

You remember how it works? The light is falling upon the book, reflecting, going into the lens of your eyes, and projected as an inverted image on your retina—you know the whole story. So, you are actually seeing the book *within* yourself.

Where do you see the whole world?

Again, within yourself.

Everything that ever happened to you, you experienced
right within you. Light and darkness, pain and pleasure,
agony and ecstasy—all of it happened within you. If someone
touches your hand right now, you may think you are experiencing their hand, but the fact of the matter is you are only
experiencing the sensations in your own hand. The whole experience is contained within. *All human experience is one
hundred percent self-created*.

If your thought and your emotion are of your making, you
can mold them any way you like. There is scientific proof
today that without ingesting a drop of alcohol or any other
substance, you can get fully intoxicated by yourself. An Is-
raeli organic chemist, Raphael Mechoulam, and his research
team initiated a project that eventually isolated a "bliss molecule" in the human system. In lay terms, they discovered
that the human brain has natural cannabis receptors. Why is
this so? They found that this is simply because the body is
capable of producing its own narcotic. It can manufacture its
own bliss with no external stimulus—and that too, with no
hangover! The reason why certain chemical substances, like
alcohol and recreational drugs, are dangerous is because they
can reduce your awareness, ruin your health, create addic-
tions, and destroy you. But here is a bliss narcotic that is created and consumed by your own system—and which has a
tremendous impact on health and well-being! It means that
the human system is wonderfully self-contained. Other similar chemicals have been discovered more recently as well, but
this particular chemical has been named "anandamide,"
based on the Sanskrit word *ananda,* which means bliss. We
can infer from this that happiness is just a certain kind of

chemistry. Peace is another kind of chemistry. In fact, every kind of pleasantness that we experience—whether peace or joy or ecstasy—is a kind of chemistry. The yogic system has always known this.

There is a technology for inner well-being—for creating a chemical basis for a blissful existence. This is one dimension of what I call "Inner Engineering." If you are aware, you can activate your system in such a way that simply breathing is an enormous pleasure. All it takes is a willingness to pay a little attention to the inner mechanism.

This is the fundamental shift in understanding that has to happen. Do not look for a way out of misery. Do not look for a way out of suffering. There is only one way—and that is *in*.

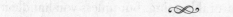

Most people think peace and joy are the goals of the spiritual life. This is a fallacy. Peace and joy are the basic requirements for a life of well-being. If you want to enjoy your dinner tonight, you must be peaceful and happy. If you want to enjoy your family, the work that you do, the world that you live in, you must be peaceful and happy. Peace and joy are not things you attain at the end of life. They are the basis of your life. If you consider peace to be the ultimate goal, you will only "rest in peace"!

The word "spirituality" is one of the most corrupted words on the planet. Don't walk the spiritual path for peace. It is because most people are so deprived of peace that they consider it to be the ultimate aspiration. When I was in Tel Aviv some years ago, I was told that *shalom* was the highest form of greeting possible. I asked why. "Because it means peace," I was told. I said, "Why would peace be the highest aspiration unless you're in the Middle East?"

If you were on a desert island without food for ten days and suddenly God appeared before you, would you want Him to appear as a shining light or in the form of bread? In India certain communities worship food as God because they have been deprived of food for a long time. In California, love is God! Whatever you feel deprived of looks like the highest aspiration. The thing to remember is that none of these will settle you in any enduring way. Human life is longing for unlimited expansion, and that is the *only* thing that will settle you for good.

The spiritual quest is not a cultivated choice. It is not an induced quest. It is a natural longing. But unless you handle it consciously, it will not yield. When being peaceful, blissful, and joyous are not efforts anymore, you naturally start seeking, want to know the nature of life. Mysticism on this planet evolved only in those places where people learned the technology of being ecstatic by their own nature. This is because only when you are blissful will you be in the highest state of receptivity, and truly willing to explore all aspects of life. Otherwise, you would not dare, because if keeping yourself pleasant is a big challenge, you can't take on other challenges.

Once it happened . . . An eighty-five-year-old man went fishing in Louisiana. When he was just about to call it a day, he caught a frog. He was about to release it into the marsh again, when the frog spoke. "Just kiss me passionately," it said, "and I will turn into a beautiful young woman."

The old man inspected the frog for a long time. The frog

puckered up its lips in anticipation. Then the old man put the frog into his fish bag.

The frog screamed, "Didn't you hear me? Just one kiss and I will turn into a really beautiful young woman!"

The old man said, "At my age, there's not much I can do with a beautiful young woman. If kissing you could turn me into a handsome young prince, that would be different. But for now—a talking frog! Believe me, I can smell money!"

Choices that you make out of inability are not life solutions. An inability to be joyful by your own nature can make the simplest issues in life seem like highly complex problems. Right now being peaceful and joyful is made out to be the most significant problem in human existence. In pursuit of human happiness, we are ripping the planet apart.

The reason the simple things—like being peaceful, joyful, loving—have become ultimate aspirations is that people are living without paying any attention to the life process. When most people say "life," they mean the accessories of life—their work, their family, their relationships, the homes they live in, the cars they drive, the clothes they wear, or the gods they pray to. The one thing they miss is *life*—the life process itself, the essential life that is you. The moment you make this fundamental mistake of identifying something that is not you as yourself, life becomes an unnecessary struggle. The foundations of peace and bliss are not about attending to the external realities of your life, but in accessing and organizing the inner nature of your being.

You are capable of experiencing only that which is within the boundaries of your sensation. But if you throw the boundary of your sensation out in an expanded form, you can sit here and experience everyone as yourself. You can stretch it further and experience the very cosmos as you experience your own body.

When this sense of inclusiveness happened to me, I understood that being loving and compassionate is not an idea. To live in empathy is not some esoteric principle. This is the way a human being is *made*. If you do not identify with anything you have accumulated over a period of time, *including your body and mind,* you will be able to experience this.

Enlightenment is not an attainment or an achievement. It is a homecoming. Your senses give you the impression that you are experiencing the outside, but you have never experienced the outside. When you realize that all that you experience is within, that absolute homecoming is enlightenment.

My life is just devoted to evolving methods so that people can experience this inclusiveness. If we truly have to create solutions that are relevant for all, an experience of absolute inclusiveness has to happen to humanity. And it is possible.

The reason why everyone is not naturally enlightened is simply this: people have categorized the world into good and bad, God and Devil, high and low, sacred and filthy, pure and impure, heaven and hell. These are parallel lines that will never meet.

Once you have fractured this existence within yourself, there is no way to reach a state of enduring well-being and freedom. You have been told to love your enemy. If you first label someone your enemy and then try to love him or her, it's going to be torturous! Once you have fragmented creation like this, there is no way to arrive at a state of absolute inclusiveness.

The problem is that human beings have lost a fundamental distinction—between inward and outward, between their way of *being* and the way they *transact* with the external world. Transactions are different, according to the nature of a situation or relationship. However remote or intimate, transactions are always governed by laws or norms.

But when it comes to our inner nature, there is only one governing principle: *borderless unity*. Our physical and social worlds are governed by boundaries. Our inner world needs none. To attain the ecstasy of borderless unity, which is our natural state, all you need to do is live by the guideline that all human experience is generated from within—either with the support of external stimuli or without. That is all. If you establish this within yourself absolutely, the consequences of your transactions will no longer be burdensome.

What do we mean by this? People often ask me, "Maybe this is possible for you as a yogi, but how can we who live in the 'real world' make our interactions free of friction?" I remind them that I don't live in a cave. I also lead people. I am doing work around the world with over three million volunteers. This means they usually aren't trained for the job they are doing—*and* you can't fire them! Do you know how difficult it is to manage such a situation? By implication, my life should be the most burdensome! But you won't ever see me distressed because my way of being is not in any way enslaved to what's happening outside. This is not an otherworldly achievement. It is possible for everyone to live this way.

If you still believe that someone "up there" is going to rescue you and solve all your problems, just remember that you are living on a round planet—and one that's spinning. So, whenever you look up, you are obviously looking in the wrong direction! In this vast ever-expanding cosmos, what's up and what's down? You have no clue. Nowhere in the cosmos is it marked "This side up"! The only distinction you do know right now is "within" and "without" (although, for the yogi, even this distinction has vanished).

Thousands of years ago, a yogi appeared in the upper reaches of the Himalayas. He came to be known as Adiyogi, the first yogi. And it was he who bequeathed the science of yoga to seven disciples, who later carried it around the world. What he imparted to these disciples was an unimaginably profound system of self-exploration and transformation, based on the radical premise that it is possible for a human being to evolve *consciously*. Unlike biological evolution, which happens without our conscious participation, spiritual evolution can happen consciously. All it takes, Adiyogi told us, is willingness.

If we were to distill the essence of his wisdom in a few lines, it would be just this. Up and down, good and bad, sacred and profane: these are all assumed. But inward and outward: this is the one context we are sure of, the one context we can work with. This is Adiyogi's most significant contribution to humankind and it is a profound and enduring one: "The only way out is *in*."

Once it happened . . . Someone came looking for the Isha Yoga Center in southern India. They came to a nearby village and asked a local boy, "How far is the Isha Yoga Center?"

The boy scratched his head and said, "24,996 miles."

The man was aghast. "What? That far?"

The boy said, "Yes, the way you're going. But if you turn around, it's just four miles."

If you go outward, it is an endless journey. If you turn inward, it is just one moment.

In that one moment, everything changes. In that one moment, you are not in pursuit of joy anymore. Instead, your life becomes *an expression* of your joyfulness.

Design Your Destiny

I was once at an international conference on how to alleviate poverty on the planet. There were several eminent participants in positions of public responsibility, including a generous sprinkling of Nobel laureates.

At one point, a participant said, "Why are we trying to solve these problems? Isn't all this divine will?"

And I said, "Yes, if somebody else is dying, somebody else is hungry, it must be divine will. But if *your* stomach is empty, if *your* child is dying of hunger, you'll have your own plan, won't you?"

Whenever we have had to do something about *our* lives, we have taken it into our hands. Whenever it comes to other people's misfortunes, we have a word to explain it: destiny.

And what a convenient word that is. Destiny has become a popular scapegoat, a way to deal with failure, a fatalistic ruse to reconcile ourselves to all kinds of uncomfortable situations. But turning inward is the first step from passivity to agency—from being a victim toward becoming a master of your own destiny.

A variety of diseases that people believed to be "God's will" until a hundred years ago, are in our hands today. This is because we have taken charge of certain situations. Polio is an example. The very word "polio" would strike terror in the hearts of many in recent history. When I was growing up, I saw quite a few polio-afflicted people about my age, in school and in my neighborhood, who were doomed to live out their lives in wheelchairs. It was a common sight, and it was an acknowledged fact that they would never be able to walk in their lives. Their affliction was usually seen as an act of God or destiny.

At the start of the twentieth century, polio was the most feared ailment in industrialized countries, irreversibly paralyzing thousands of children. Effective vaccines helped practically eliminate this disease in the 1950s and '60s. When it was recognized as a major problem in developing countries, immunization programs were introduced. In 1988, polio afflicted 350,000 children around the world in a single year; in 2013, the number had dropped to 416. By 2012, India was no longer on the list of polio-endemic countries. A combination of political advocacy, public and private partnerships, effective reasonably priced vaccines, community participation, and teams of global healthcare workers, proved that despite all the obstacles, even in a country as vast and challenging as India, eradication *was* possible.

To be human means you can mold situations you are living in the way you want them. But today most people in the world are molded by the situations in which they exist. This is simply because they live in reaction to situations they are placed in. The inevitable question is, "Why was I placed in such a situation? Isn't it my destiny?" Whatever we do not want to take responsibility for, whatever we cannot make sense of logically, we label "destiny." It is a consoling word, but disempowering.

To mold situations the way you want them you must first know who you are. The crux of the matter is that you don't yet know who you are. Who you are is not the sum total of accumulations you have made. Everything that you currently know as "myself" is just an accumulation. Your body is just an accumulation of food. Your mind is just an accumulation of impressions gathered through the five senses. What you accumulate can be yours, but it can never be you.

Who then *are* you? That is yet to come into your experience. That is still in an unconscious state. You are trying to live your life through what you have gathered, not through who you *are*. What's more, you are not even a hundred percent conscious of what you have gathered!

You have acquired certain tendencies over the years, depending on the impressions you have accumulated. These can be transformed entirely. If you do a certain amount of inner work, if you implement certain inner technologies— irrespective of your current tendencies, your past experience of life, your genetics, your environment—you can completely rewire yourself in a short span of time!

Everything in this existence is happening naturally according to a certain organic law. If you know the nature of life within you, you can completely take charge of the way it happens, but within the broad parameters set by the laws of nature. What do we mean by this? Let us look at a concrete example. Although we are wingless creatures, we have still, in the last one hundred years, managed to fly. How? Not by breaking the laws of nature, but through a deeper understanding of the laws of nature. So, the technology we are going to explore in this book is a small part of the much deeper science that eventually enables an adept to take the very process of life and death into his or her hands.

Your destiny is written by you *unconsciously*. If you have mastery over your physical body, fifteen to twenty percent of your life and destiny will be in your hands. If you have mastery over your mind, fifty to sixty percent of your life and destiny will be in your hands. If you have mastery over your life energies, *a hundred percent* of your life and destiny will be in your hands.

Even now you are choosing your life, but you are choosing it in total unawareness. But whatever you do in unawareness, you can also do in awareness. That makes a world of a difference. It is the difference between ignorance and enlightenment.

Unpleasantness is happening to you, in the form of anger, fear, anxiety, and stress, because your basic faculties—your body, mind, and life energies—are doing their own thing. When mind and body exist only to serve the life within you, why is your life currently enslaved to the mind and body? Isn't this a complete distortion of the way life should function?

Taking destiny into your hands doesn't mean everything will happen your way. The outside world will never happen a hundred percent your way, because there are too many variables involved. Wanting the outside to happen exactly the way you choose is the path of conquest, tyranny, dictatorship.

Once it happened . . . Shankaran Pillai (a certain South

Indian gentleman you met in the introduction and will meet several times more in the course of this book) went drinking with his buddies. He thought he would have a quick drink and go home at eight o'clock. And so he did. He had a quick drink, and a quick drink, and another quick drink. And then one more quick drink. He looked at his watch. It said two thirty. (Drink makes people like yogis—timeless.) He got off the barstool. It is such an unfair world: a man is expected to walk on a round planet that spins. With great skill and dexterity, he balanced himself and started making his journey homeward.

Taking a shortcut through a park, he fell headlong into a rosebush. His face became a mess. He gathered himself and started making his way again. In this condition, he reached home, and tried to find the keyhole. But those wretched keyholes nowadays are made so small! That took another twenty minutes.

He finally got in and stumbled into the bedroom. Fortunately, the wife was a big sleeper. He went into the bathroom, looked at himself in the mirror. His face was a real mess. He opened the medicine cabinet, took out some medicine and a box of Band-Aids and fixed himself, whichever way he could. Then he crawled quietly into bed.

Next morning, his wife threw a bucket of cold water on his face.

He woke up gasping, feeling water-boarded. He said, "Why, why? It's only a Sunday!"

She said, "You fool! Once again drinking?"

"No, honey, I promised you six months ago. Since then, I haven't touched a drop."

She held him by the shirt, dragged him into the bathroom, and showed him: the Band-Aids were all over the mirror!

When pain, misery, or anger happen, it is time to look within you, not around you. To achieve well-being the only one who needs to be fixed is *you*. What you forget is that when you are sick, it is *you* who needs the medication. When you are hungry, it is *you* who needs the food. The only one that needs to be fixed is you, but just to understand this simple fact people take lifetimes!

Creating your own destiny does not mean you have to control every situation in the world. Creating your destiny is about steadily heading toward your well-being and your ultimate nature, no matter what the content of life is around you. It simply means making yourself in such a way that, whatever the events and situations around you, you don't get crushed by them; *you ride them.*

The spiritual process is not about imposing your ideas on existence; it is about making yourself in such a way that the creation and the Creator, and every atom in this existence, cannot help yielding to you. When you pursue your own likes and dislikes, you feel alone in this vast existence, constantly insecure, unstable, psychologically challenged. But once existence yields to you, it delivers you to a different place of grace—where every pebble, every rock, every tree, every atom, speaks to you in a language you understand. Every moment there are a million miracles happening around you: a flower blossoming, a bird tweeting, a bee humming, a raindrop falling, a snowflake wafting along the clear evening air. There is magic everywhere. If you learn how to live it, life is nothing short of a daily miracle.

It doesn't matter who you are, life doesn't work for you unless you do the right things. You may consider yourself a good person, but if you don't water your garden, will it flower? You need to do the right things if you want results. Judgments about good and bad are essentially human and socially conditioned. These are fine as social norms. But existence is not concerned with these conclusions. Existence is not judgmental. It treats all of us the same way.

One winter morning in Michigan, an old-timer went ice-fishing. It was ten o'clock in the morning. He cut a small hole in the ice and sat down with a crate of beer beside him. Fishing is not just about the catch; it is a patience game. He knew that. He put the line in. One by one, the beer cans started emptying out. The fishing basket also stayed empty.

The day drew on. At four o'clock in the afternoon, his basket was still empty. So was his crate of beer.

A young boy came along. He was carrying a big boom box that played deafening heavy metal music. He cut a hole in the ice nearby, and sat down to fish, his music still blaring.

The old-timer glanced at him with ill-disguised contempt. "I've been sitting here since morning quietly, with not a single fish, and the fool thinks he can catch fish with music blaring, at four in the afternoon! No fool like a young fool!"

To his amazement, within ten minutes, the boy landed a huge trout! The old man dismissed it as a lucky break and continued fishing. Ten minutes later the boy caught one more big trout.

Now the old man could ignore it no longer. He stared at

the boy, dumbfounded. And just then, to his utter disbelief, the boy landed one more huge trout.

The old-timer cast his pride aside and walked slowly over to the boy. "What is the secret?" he asked. "I've been sitting here the whole day and my basket is empty. You already have three huge trout. What's going on?"

The boy said, "Ru ra ra ra ru ra rum."

The old man put his hand to his ear and asked, "What?"

The boy turned down the stereo and said, "Ru ra ra ra ru ra rum."

The old man was perplexed. "I don't understand a word you're saying."

The boy spat a blob of something into his hand and said, "You have to keep the worms warm."

Unless you do the right things, the right things will not happen to you. Principles and philosophies are only of social consequence. It is time to wake up to yourself as an existential being, a living being, rather than a psychological case. Then your destiny will be your own. One hundred percent your own.

This is not an idle promise. It is a guarantee.

No Boundary, No Burden

Once it happened . . . An argument arose one evening between a husband and wife. The argument was over the burning question: who should close the front door today?

Not a simple question. And not a laughing matter. These are very serious issues in domestic situations. Who should close the door today, who should switch off the garden lights this evening, who should take the dog for a walk—these are questions that can drive couples to divorce.

The argument grew more and more heated. The wife decided, "Every day, it is I who in the end accepts defeat. Today, I am not going to give in." The husband also grew equally determined. "She pushes me around all the time. I am not going to give in to this woman today, no matter what."

It was one of those grand rows. Now, every home has its own system of resolving these arguments. In this family, when confronted by an impasse, both husband and wife would sit silently; the person who uttered the first word would have to go and close the door.

The two sat in stony silence. Minutes ticked on into hours.

Dinner was on the table. If the husband said he wanted to eat, he would have to close the door. If the wife proposed dinner, she would have to close the door.

Midnight. They were still sitting. A few rogues were passing by on the street. They saw the doors of the house open, lights on, no party, nothing. Everything was quiet. They wanted to see what was going on, so they looked into the sitting room. They saw two people sitting there, steadfastly silent.

The rogues looked at the silent couple. They were a little surprised. They decided to take a chance. They helped themselves to a few valuables in the sitting room. The two people said nothing. The rogues grew amused. Emboldened, they sat at the dining table and served themselves dinner. The couple sat heroically silent.

The rogues were hugely tickled. What the hell was happening here? They grew bolder still. One of them kissed the wife. Still, the couple didn't utter a word. The one who spoke would have to close the door. The stakes were too high. Neither could risk it.

Now the rogues got a bit spooked. They decided it was time to leave this strange household. But before they left, they wanted to leave their mark. They decided to shave off the husband's moustache. One of them approached him, razor in hand.

Then the husband finally spoke. He said, "Okay, damn it, I'll close the door!"

Perhaps the scenarios are different, but are there not situations in your life that hinge on a similar question: who's responsible?

Who *is* responsible?

It's a big question. Let's put the question more precisely: who is responsible for the way you are right now?

Your genes? Your father? Your mother? Your wife? Your husband? Your teacher? Your boss? Your mother-in-law? God? The government? All of the above?

The condition is a pervasive one. Ask someone, "Why are you in this situation?" Pat comes the response, "You know, when I was a child, my parents . . ." The same old story, with just a few variations.

There is an ancient science of how to create misery, and one in which human beings need no encouragement whatsoever. There is almost no one who is not an expert. Passing the buck is what you do in a hundred different ways each day. You have collectively refined the old blame game into a fine art.

The quality of our lives is determined by our ability to respond to the varied complex situations that we encounter. If the ability to respond with intelligence, competence, and sensitivity is compromised by a compulsive or reactive approach, we are enslaved by the situation. It means we have allowed the nature of our life experience to be determined by our circumstances, not by us.

Being fully responsible is to be fully conscious. What you consider to be your body is what you have gathered through ingestion. What you consider to be your mind is what you have gathered through the five senses. What is beyond that— which you did not gather—is who you *are*. Being alive is being conscious. Everybody is conscious to some degree, but when you touch the dimension beyond body and beyond mind, you have touched that which is the very source of consciousness.

You realize then that the entire universe is conscious. You inhabit a living cosmos.

The physical and psychological dimensions belong to the realm of polarities—pain-pleasure, love-hate, masculine-feminine, and so on. If you have one, the other is bound to follow. But when you move into the fundamental dimension of who you are, you are beyond all polarities. You now become blissful by your own nature. You are the master of your own destiny.

It is time to reclaim for ourselves the extraordinary transformative power of this single word: *responsibility*. Apply it to your life, and watch the magic unfold.

Let us settle what we mean by the word, at the start. "Responsibility" is a much misunderstood term. It has been used so widely and indiscriminately that it has lost much of its inner voltage. Responsibility does not mean taking on the burdens of the world. It does not mean accepting blame for things you have done or not done. It does not mean living in a state of perpetual guilt.

Responsibility simply means your *ability to respond*. If you decide, "I am responsible," you will have the ability to respond. If you decide, "I am not responsible," you will not have the ability to respond. It is as simple as that. All it requires is for you to realize that you are responsible for all that you are and all that you are not, all that may happen to you and all that may not happen to you.

This is not a mind game. This is not a self-help strategy for easy living. This is not a philosophical theory. This is a reality. Your physical existence is possible only because of your body's seamless ability to respond to the entire universe. If your body wasn't responding, you wouldn't be able to exist for a moment. Do you see that?

What the trees around you are exhaling, you are inhaling right now; what you are exhaling, the trees are inhaling at this very moment. This transaction is ongoing. Whether you are aware of it or not, one half of your pulmonary system is hanging up there right now on a tree! You have never experienced this interdependence; you have probably, at the most, thought about it intellectually. But if you had experienced this connection, would anyone have to tell you, "Plant trees, protect the forests, save the world"? Would it even be necessary?

Taking responsibility is not a convenient philosophy to reconcile you to the way things are. It is simply waking up to reality. This ability to respond to the entire universe is already a physical reality. It is only your thoughts and emotions that need to become conscious of the fact.

Suppose something goes wrong in your office. Perhaps you think it was due to a particular colleague's ineptitude. You could haul her up, lose your temper, fire her. Your blood pressure is likely to rise; the office atmosphere will be vitiated; the aftereffects of your rage will probably be felt by you and your fellow workers for days and weeks after the incident; you will probably have to work particularly hard at restoring the peace and reestablishing a situation of mutual trust.

There is another choice. You could simply see the situation the way it is and take responsibility for it. Taking responsibility is not accepting blame instead of assigning it. It simply means consciously responding to the situation. Once you take responsibility, you will invariably start exploring ways to address the situation. You will look for solutions.

If you are frequently in this mode, your ability to craft your life situations will keep enhancing itself. With this enhanced competence to deal with life and its multiple complexities, you begin to rise to positions of possibility and power. If you assume absolute responsibility within yourself for all that is around you, you will become the center of any situation at home, work, or even the universe. Since you become indispensable to these situations, there is no sense of insecurity or incompleteness within you anymore.

Only if you realize you are responsible do you have the freedom to create yourself the way you want to be, not as a reaction to the situations in which you exist. *Reactivity is enslavement. Responsibility is freedom.* When you are able to create yourself the way you want, you can create your life the way you want as well. Your outer life may not be a hundred percent in your control, but your inner life always will.

On the other hand, the first reaction—anger—usually provokes unintelligent action. Anger is fundamentally self-defeating. If you look at your life closely, you will find that you have done the most idiotic and life-negative things when you were angry. Above all, you were working against yourself. If you work against yourself, if you sabotage your own well-being, you are obviously choosing unintelligence as a way of life.

I am not propounding a moral argument here. I am not telling you that you should not lose your temper because it is ethically wrong. If anger is a pleasant experience, blow your top. What's the problem? The point is it is singularly unpleasant—for you and for those at the receiving end. It is also counterproductive and therefore inefficient.

I am not offering a rage-control or anger management strategy either. When I first came to the United States, I heard everybody talking about "stress management." It puzzled me. Why would anybody want to *manage* stress? I always thought we managed the things that are precious to us—our money, our business, our family. It took me time to see that people have assumed that stress is an inevitable part of their lives! They do not see that it is entirely self-created and self-inflicted. Once you take charge of your inner life, *there is no such thing as stress*.

The point is that anger is rooted in your false perception that you can change the situation by losing your temper with it. But your life experience tells you time and again that the reverse is true, that you can never change any situation for the better by forsaking your sense and intelligence. You only mess up your situations by getting angry. Once you see that clearly, you've taken the first step toward change.

Besides, there is substantial medical and scientific evidence to prove that in a state of anger, you are literally poisoning your system. This can be verified with something as simple as a blood test. When you are angry, your very chemistry is altered, and your system turns toxic. Intense activity and sleep are times when this chemical mess can undo itself. But if you are in frequent states of rage, you are heading toward physical and psychological disaster. There is no doubt about this.

There is a commonly held belief that rage produces results; that nothing happens in the world without the adrenaline rush of anger. The iconic figure of the Cuban revolution, Che Guevara, famously said, "If you tremble with indignation at every injustice, you are a comrade of mine." Perhaps that is true. But *in* rage, you become one with a group; *out* of rage, you become one with the universe.

∝∞⌖

Once it happened . . . A gentleman carrying an infant was traveling from London to Bristol on a train. Another gentleman entered the compartment, dumped his two huge suitcases, and sat beside the first.

As you know, Englishmen don't immediately speak to each other. So, the first gentleman waited very politely for a while. Then he turned to the second passenger and said, "Looking at your suitcases, I presume you are a salesperson? I am also one."

The gentleman said, "Yes, I am a salesman."

Another genteel pause. Then the first passenger asked, "What do you sell?"

The other replied, "I sell helical gears." Another decorous silence. Then he asked the first gentleman, "And what do *you* sell?"

He said, "I sell condoms."

Shocked, the second gentleman said, "You sell condoms and you are taking your son with you on your business? Is that appropriate?"

"This is not my son," replied the first passenger. "It's a complaint from Bristol."

Human beings are in a perennial state of complaint. They

carry their complaints with them like a badge of their identity. There are many who live their lives lamenting that life has been particularly unfair to them. They cite instances of all the terrible things that have befallen them, the chances they never got, the many injustices they have suffered. Maybe it is even true.

What most people forget is that the past exists within each one of us *only as memory*. Memory has no objective existence. It is not existential; it is purely psychological. If you retain your ability to respond, your memory of the past will become an empowering process. But if you are in a compulsive cycle of reactivity, memory distorts your perception of the present, and your thoughts, emotions, and actions become disproportionate to the stimulus.

The choice is always before you: to *respond consciously* to the present; or to *react compulsively* to it. There is a vast difference between the two. And it can make the world of a difference.

If terrible things have happened to you, you ought to have grown wise. If the worst possible events have befallen you, you should be the wisest of the lot. But instead of growing wise, most people become wounded. In a state of conscious response, it is possible to use every life situation—however ugly—as an opportunity for growth. But if you habitually think, "I am the way I am because of someone else," you are using life situations merely as an opportunity for self-destruction or stagnation.

I once heard a moving account of a woman who used one of the most horrific life situations to transform herself into a beautiful being. In the beginning of the Second World War, a bunch of Nazi soldiers broke into a house in Austria. They took the adults away separately, and the two children—a thirteen-year-old girl and an eight-year-old boy—were taken to a railway station. As they waited along with other children for the train to arrive, the boys started a game. Oblivious to what lay in store, they started playing, as children are wont to do.

A cargo train arrived and the soldiers started packing everyone into it. Once they were in, the little girl noticed that her brother had forgotten to bring his shoes. It was an Austrian winter, a bitter one. Without shoes, you could lose your feet. The girl lost her temper. She shook her kid brother, boxed his ears, and abused him. "You idiot! Don't we have enough trouble on our hands? We don't know where our parents are, we don't know where we're going! And now you go and lose your shoes? What am I supposed to do with you?"

At the next station, the boys and girls were separated. And that is the last that the brother and sister ever saw of each other.

About three and a half years later, the girl came out of the concentration camp. She discovered she was the only one alive in her family. Everyone else had vanished, including her brother. All that remained was the memory of the harsh words she had uttered the last time she had seen him alive.

That was when she made a life-changing decision: "It doesn't matter who I meet, I will never speak to them in a manner that I regret later, because this meeting could be my last." She could have spent her life in defeat and remorse, but she made this simple decision, which transformed her life phenomenally. She went on to live a rich and fulfilled life.

The most horrific things in life can be a source of nourishment if you accept, "I am responsible for the way I am now." It is possible to transform the greatest adversity into a stepping-stone for personal growth. If you take one hundred percent responsibility for the way you are now, a brighter tomorrow is a possibility. But if you take no responsibility for the present—if you blame your parents, your friend, your husband, your girlfriend, your colleagues for the way you are— you have forsaken your future even before it comes.

You come into this world with nothing and you go empty-handed. The wealth of life lies only in how you have allowed its experiences to enrich you. Filth can blossom into the fragrance of a flower. Manure can transform itself into the sweetness of a mango. No adversity is an impediment if you are in a state of conscious response. No matter what the nature of the situation you are in, it can only enhance your experience of life, if you allow it to.

Resentment, anger, jealousy, pain, hurt, and depression are poisons that *you* drink but expect someone else to die. Life does not work that way. Most people take lifetimes to understand this simple truth.

Now that we have established what responsibility is, it is time to look at what it is not. Let us start by clearing up a few fundamental misconceptions.

For one, many believe that taking responsibility compromises their freedom. This seems to be logically true, on a simplistic level. Existentially, it is completely off the mark.

Let us consider a concrete scenario. Your pen falls off a table. If you see you are responsible for it, you have several choices before you. You could simply bend down and pick it up. If you are unable to do that, you could ask someone to help. Or if you aren't inclined to act on it right now, you might pick it up later. You have a variety of options.

If, on the other hand, you don't take responsibility for it, what can you do? Nothing.

Which is freedom? To have choices or to have none?

Your logical mind tells you, "Give up all responsibility and you will be free." But in your experience of life, the more you are able to respond to everything around you, the freer you are! The logical and experiential dimensions of life work in dia-metrically opposite ways. Logic is not without its uses, but these help only to handle the material aspects of life. If you handle your entire life with logic alone, you will end up a mess.

Secondly, people often confuse responsibility with reac-tion. We have already demonstrated earlier that there is a world of difference between the two. The first is born in awareness, the second in unawareness. The first is born in con-sciousness, the second in unconsciousness. The first is free-dom, the second enslavement.

It is time to make yet another distinction. Responsibility is not reaction but *it is not action* either.

Responsibility and action belong to different dimensions. The ability to respond gives you the freedom to act. It also gives you the freedom not to act. It puts you in the driver's seat of your life. It empowers you to decide the nature and volume of action you want to undertake. Responsibility is not com-pulsive action; it offers you the *choice of action*.

Can you act upon everything in the world today? No, but you can respond to everything in the world today. Action has to be judiciously performed, depending on a careful analysis of resources—strength, capability, energy, age, situation. Your ability to act is always limited, but there are no limitations on your ability to respond. If you are willing, you can respond to just about anything.

Just because you are responsible for your children, are you able to do everything for them? If you did everything for them, you would mess up their lives. Your sense of responsibility makes you do certain things for them and not do others. So, responsibility does not mean unbridled action. Far from it.

How, you may ask, are you responsible for the violence and injustice in the world? How are you responsible for the war and the bloodshed, the atrocities against the marginal and the underprivileged, all over the world? Certainly you are not to blame for any of it. But the moment you become conscious of any of these events, you do respond—either in concern, love, care, hate, anger, indignation, or even action. It is just that this is often an unconscious reaction rather than a conscious response. If you make this ability to respond into a willing process, that marks the birth of a tremendous new possibility within you. Your inner genius begins to flower.

Can you then respond to the moon? You can. Your body and life energies certainly do. When entire oceans rise in response to the cycles of the moon, do you think the water content in your own system doesn't rise as well? Maybe you aren't an astronaut; maybe you can never walk on the moon. But you can respond to the moon. In fact, you already do. You can just choose to do it—willingly, consciously.

And that brings us to the fourth misconception. Many think responsibility means capability.

Wrong again. When it comes to action, capability could play a role. But when it comes to response, it is just a question of willingness.

If you see someone dying on the street, are you responsible?

If you are willing to respond, you will explore various options. If you are a doctor, you will try direct intervention. If you are not, you may call an ambulance. Or if all this is being done by someone else, you will at least have concern in your heart. But if you are not responsible, you will just sit there like a stone watching someone die before your eyes.

Your ability to respond is the way you *are*. Only your ability to act is connected with the outside world. Responsibility is not about talking, thinking, or doing. Responsibility is about *being*. That's the way life is—not an independent, self-contained bubble but a moment-to-moment dialogue with the universe. You don't have to work at making it that way. You just have to see it the way it is.

Let us deepen the exploration. If responsibility is "response-ability," the capacity to be responsive to situations, let me ask you another question: is your ability to respond limited or limitless?

Are you capable of responding to a plant?

You are.

To a stranger on the street?

You are.

To the moon?

You are.

To the sun, to the stars?

You are.

To the whole cosmos?

You are.

In fact, as we have seen, every subatomic particle in your body is responding in a limitless way to the great dance of energies that is the cosmos. The only reason you are not experiencing the life process in all its majesty and profundity is your current state of mental resistance. Your psychological structure is a stone wall. If you are willing, every moment of your life can be a fantastic experience. Just the act of inhaling and exhaling can be a tremendous love affair.

Why is the mind resisting this?

Because it is crippled by its own limited logic which says, "Taking responsibility for just two people already gives me a headache. If I take responsibility for the whole world what will happen? I'll crack up!"

Through millions of years of evolution, nature has caged you within certain boundaries—this is the human predicament. But this imprisonment is only on the level of biology. On the level of human consciousness, you are like a bird in a cage without a door. What a tragic irony! It is only out of long aeons of habit that you are refusing to fly free.

Life has left everything open for you. Existence has not blocked anything for anyone. If you are willing, you can access the whole universe. Someone said, "Knock and it shall open." You don't even have to knock, because there *is* no door. It is open. You just have to walk through, that's all.

This is the sole purpose of the spiritual process. The life and work of every spiritual guide, across history and across culture, has been just this: to point out that the cage door does not exist. Whether you fly or choose to remain in the limitations of the cage—let that be a conscious choice.

The possibility of ultimate freedom may seem deeply threatening to many. Yes, it is a threat—but only to your limitations. Do you want to live a life of voluntary self-imprisonment? Limiting your responsibility is to suffocate yourself on various levels—physically, intellectually, and emotionally. Unfortunately, this stifling of life is understood by people as safety, as security.

Take the case of a seed. If the seed constantly tries to save itself, a new life is impossible. The seed goes through the tremendous struggle of losing what it believes is its identity—losing its safety and integrity and becoming vulnerable—in order to grow into a many-branched leafy tree, abundant in fruit and flower. But without that vulnerability, that voluntary openness to transformation, life won't sprout.

One of the biggest problems in the world today is loneliness. It is quite incredible. The planet is teeming with seven billion people, but people are lonely! If someone enjoys being alone, there is no problem at all. But most people are suffering because of it! They are going through serious psychological problems as a consequence. If you are lonely, it is because you have chosen to become an island unto yourself. It doesn't have to be this way. "I am not responsible" makes you unwilling to get along with anyone—until you can't even get along with yourself. It often comes to a point when you believe you are not even responsible for what is happening within yourself!

What the mind forgets is that the ability to respond is *the basis of life*. If the ability is acknowledged willingly, you become blissful. If it happens unwillingly, you become miserable.

Being responsible is taking ownership of your life. It means you have taken the first radical step to becoming a complete human being—fully conscious and fully human. In taking responsibility and beginning the journey toward conscious living, you are putting an end to the age-old patterns of assigning blame outward or heavenward. You have begun the greatest adventure life has to offer: the voyage inward.

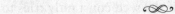

This notion of responsibility, as you might have noticed, seems to lead us seamlessly to another word, remarkably similar in its implications. A word we know well. Perhaps much too well. A much-used, much-abused four-letter word.

Love.

You know the teachings, of course. All over the world, people have been told that love is the ultimate, love is supreme, love is divine, that we must love our neighbors, and so on. All wonderful teachings. But when you *try* to become loving, it is difficult and often ends up seeming pretentious. Have you noticed this? It seems easier to not love at all than to try to become loving!

But to be loving is simply this: a willingness to respond freely and openly. Right now, it may be limited to one or two people in your lives. But it is possible to extend this ability to embrace the entire world.

Does it mean going out into the streets and hugging everyone? No. That would be crazy—not to mention, irresponsible. As we have said, responsibility is not about action, but a way of being. *Love is not something you do; it is just the way you are.*

Right now, you have left one window in your life open—for a few people. You did that because somewhere you understood that if you closed that window, you'd go mad. Your only options would be insanity or suicide. But there is another way to approach this. Does it mean opening another window? Or opening a door?

Here's a more effective option: why don't you just demolish the wall?

Love has nothing to do with someone else. It is all about *you*. It is a way of being. It essentially means you have brought sweetness into your emotion. If a loved one travels to another country, would you still be able to love them? You would. If a loved one passed away, would you still be able to love them? You would. Even if a loved one is not physically with you anymore, you are still capable of being loving. So, what *is* love then? It is just your own quality. You are only using the other person as a key to open up what is already within you.

Why are you fumbling with keys when there is no lock, when there is no door, when there is no wall? You create illusory walls and doors and then create illusory keys—and then you fumble with the keys! And once you find the key, you are terrified of losing it!

For most people, love is initially a joy, but after a while it becomes an anxiety. Why? Because this "key" has legs and a will of its own. You can't keep it in your pocket or hang it around your neck. When you try to do that, two lives are heading straight for disaster!

Once your joy is on self-start rather than push-start, you have upgraded your technology. You are no longer enslaved to an external source—whether a person or a situation. You are now capable of being loving and blissful without doing anything in particular, just sitting here, no matter how anyone in the outside world behaves. Once you experience this inner freedom, you will never experience insecurity in your life again. And anyway, when you are a truly blissful human being, everyone will naturally want to be around you! Blissfulness means life is happening in an exuberant manner, and that is all that life seeks.

So, how does one upgrade one's inner technology?

We will look at this at length in the following chapters. But a fundamental step would be to recognize consciously just this: *"My ability to respond is limitless, but my ability to act is limited. I am one hundred percent responsible for everything I am and everything I am not, for my capacities and my incapacities, for my joys and my miseries. I am the one who determines the nature of my experience in this life and beyond. I am the maker of my life."*

Absolutely nothing is required—no reaction, no action, no capability—other than being aware of the basic fact that *your responsibility is limitless*. You could sit in one place and be aware of it. You could walk the street and be aware of it. You could be working, cooking, or even lying in bed, and be aware of it.

Let me ask you another question: whatever your religion or

cultural background, what exactly do you mean when you use the word "God"?

The forms, the names, the ideas are varied. But essentially, when you say "God," you mean that which is responsible for everything in the universe. Suppose God said, "I will not be responsible for you." He is most definitely fired! The very word "God" signifies limitless responsibility.

So, responsibility is not a teaching in civics. It is *the simplest and easiest way for you to express your own divinity.*

The whole effort of the spiritual process is to break the boundaries you have drawn for yourself and experience the immensity that you are. The aim is to unshackle yourself from the limited identity you have forged, as a result of your own ignorance, and live the way the Creator made you—utterly blissful and infinitely responsible.

After my experience on Chamundi Hill, one thing became clear to me. In life, there is no "this" and "that"; there is only "this" and "this." This means everything is *here and now.* The access for everything is here and now. And it lies only in one's ability to respond—in one's ability to experience and express the divine.

There is no "yes" and "no." There is just "yes" and "yes"! The choice is yours. You can either react to life with "yes" and "no," which will mean a perpetual division of this existence, which is the basis of repetitive cycles of conflict and misery. Or you can become one big YES to life.

Limited responsibility is a way of drawing boundaries. What you think you are responsible for will be within your boundary. What you think you are not responsible for will be outside your boundary. But limitless responsibility extends itself way beyond your present level of understanding and perception. There is more—much more—to life than you are aware of right now. Once you choose to become conscious of this simple fact—*my ability to respond is limitless*—suddenly life within you reorganizes itself in a completely different way. You move into higher and higher levels of freedom within yourself. Life is now a wonderful and exhilarating journey of self-discovery.

The outside world has seen its share of bloody revolutions. They were violent because there were some people who were willing to change and there were some who were unwilling. But in the inner life, there is only one kind of revolution and it is a silent one. It is about moving from unwillingness to willingness.

The question is: do you want to be a full-time human being or a part-time human being? If you restrict your ability to respond, the scope and dimension of your experience will be unsurprising, predictable, limited, narrow. But to be an absolutely full-time human being is to be a constant full-blooded response to everything. You don't have to do anything in particular. You just need to become a willing piece of life in this glorious living cosmos.

Responsibility is not burdensome. Boundaries are burdensome. If you draw yourself a boundary, whether of ideology, caste, creed, race, or religion, you cannot move beyond it and you end up stuck for no reason at all. These boundaries only end up breeding fear, hatred, and anger. The bigger your boundary, the more burdensome it becomes. But if your responsibility is limitless, where's the boundary?

No boundary, no burden.

This is the turnaround in human consciousness that needs to take place.

Once this happens, it is not that the cosmos begins to happen your way. Instead, what *you* are becomes cosmic.

This is not transcendence; this is homecoming.

Sadhana

Don't simply believe what you are reading. The only way to find out whether something is true or untrue is to experiment with it. Stop the internal debate and simply put it to the test. The yogic path is not a path of inherited belief; it is the path of experiment.

Here's a practical way to begin.

When you have your next meal, do not talk to anyone around you for the first fifteen minutes. Just be in active conscious response to the food that you eat, the air that you breathe, the water that you drink.

As I have said earlier, your entire system is responding anyway. Just become conscious of it. This apple, this carrot, this piece of bread—don't take them lightly. If you do not eat for a couple of days, you won't think about God. You will only think about food. This is what is nourishing you and making your life right now. This is the very substance of your body. Respond to food absolutely, with total attention.

This fruit, this egg, this bread, this vegetable—they are all a part of life themselves, but they are willing to become you. Would you be willing to do this for anyone? You are not willing to lose your identity and merge into anyone. You are not even willing to surrender your little finger for someone else. Momentarily, you surrender just a little, usually when you need something. Your love affairs are the product of very calculated surrender. But food, which is a life unto itself, gives itself up completely to become a part of you.

Later, without even uttering the sentence aloud, take the simple idea—"My responsibility is limitless; if I am willing, I can respond to everything"—into the entire day. Be conscious of it until the last moment before you fall asleep and remind yourself of it the first thing when you wake up.

If you sustain this awareness of your limitless nature for just one full minute, you will achieve a tremendous transformation. A minute may seem very simple, but you will see it will take a certain level of application to arrive at this. Just one minute can elevate you to a different dimension of experience and function. Right now, your awareness is erratic: this moment you are aware and the next moment, you are gone. It is okay. Every hour, remind yourself. Experiment with this awareness, allow it to deepen and see what happens.

Conscious response brings you to a profound and enduring state of connectedness with life—not as an idea or an emotion, but life as life is. In this willing, active involvement with life, you are embraced by it and that embrace takes you to the very source of creation.

That is all it takes to touch the Creator—just willingness, nothing else.

"... And Now, Yoga"

Patanjali's *Yoga Sutras,* one of the most profound documents on the yogic sciences, begins with a strange line: "... And now, yoga."

A great document on life starts with just half a sentence! Why?

This is because you arrive at yoga only when you realize that your desire is essentially for the limitless, and that absolutely nothing else will settle you. Every human being lives in a perpetual state of insufficiency. No matter who you are or what you have achieved, you still want a little more than what you have right now. This is human desire. But the fundamental desire within every human being is for boundless expansion.

Most people are not aware of the nature of their longing. When their longing finds *unconscious* expression, we call this greed, conquest, ambition. When their longing finds *conscious* expression, we call this yoga.

If you still believe that everything will be okay the moment you find a new girlfriend or boyfriend, get a raise, buy a new house or car, then it is not yet time for yoga. Once you've tried all those things and more, and clearly know that none of it will ever be enough—*then* you are ready.

So now, yoga.

❦

What exactly *is* yoga?

If you were to close your eyes and conjure an image, it would probably be one of bodies twisted into impossible postures. Bone-bending, muscle-knotting, teeth-gnashing contortionism—that, for many, is yoga!

The trend is changing nowadays to some extent, and many yoga studios also impart breathing techniques and meditation processes. So, for some people, the image of yoga might be one of serenely smiling faces and perfect bodies seated effortlessly in lotus position.

But none of that is what we mean when we talk of *the science of yoga*.

Yoga is not a practice. It is not an exercise. It is not a technique. The images in popular consciousness point to a bowdlerized form of yoga that has now pervaded the world. This is a travesty of a science of extraordinary grandeur and profundity that originated on the Indian subcontinent.

The science of yoga is, quite simply, the science of being in perfect alignment, in absolute harmony, in complete sync with existence.

The many fluctuations of the outside world have their impact on each one of us. But yoga is the science of creating inner situations exactly the way you want them. When you fine-tune yourself to such a point where everything functions beautifully within you, naturally the best of your abilities will flow out of you.

You have surely noticed that when you are happy, you always function better. You seem to have an endless supply of energy. You can go on and on, even without eating or sleeping. Just a little happiness liberates you from your normal limitations of energy and capability.

When your body and mind are in a relaxed state, you are also free of several nagging ailments. Let's say you go and sit in your office with a headache. A headache is not a major disease. But just that throbbing can take away a whole lot of your capability at work and your enthusiasm for the job—and perhaps for life itself. A simple headache can turn what is most precious to you into a source of vexation or even misery. (This also works conversely. When your loved ones are irritated with you, they invariably feign a headache!) But with the practice of yoga, your body and mind can be maintained at the highest possible level of capability and efficiency.

And yet, yoga is not just a self-help tool for greater mental and physical efficiency—and freedom from headaches. It is all that and much more.

Modern science tells us that all of existence is just energy manifesting itself in different ways and in different forms. This means that the same energy that can sit here as a rock can lie there as mud, can stand up as a tree, can run like a dog—or be here reading this book, as you. So, you are essentially a morsel of energy that is part of the much larger energy system of the universe. The cosmos is just one big organism. Your life is not independent of it. You cannot live without the world because there is a very deep moment-to-moment transaction between the two of you.

Although everything in the universe is the same energy, it functions at different levels of capability in different forms. The same energy functions in one plant to create roses; in another plant it functions to create jasmine. With the same material with which people made earthen pots we now make computers, cars, and even spacecrafts! It is the same material; we have just started using it for higher and higher possibilities. Essentially, natural evolution is a similar phenomenon: from the same material of this planet, what an incredible journey has been made, from an amoeba to a human being!

It is the same with our inner energies. Yoga is the technology of upgrading, activating, and refining these inner energies for the highest possibilities. Suddenly, your capabilities reach a level of brilliance that you never imagined possible. An accidental and limited life turns near-miraculous.

But yoga performs an even deeper function than ensuring well-being at body, mind, and energy levels. Literally, yoga means "union." When you are in yoga, it means that in your experience, everything has become one. This is the essence of the science. This is also its deepest aim.

What is this union? What unites with what?

Right now, you are aware of someone called "me" and someone called the "other." This "me" and "other" can be extended to groups of people, communities, and nations, but fundamentally "me" and "other" is the basis of conflict in the universe. The whole point of yoga is to bring you to an experience wherein, if you sit here, there is no such thing as "you" and "me." It is all me—or all you! Any process that helps you to reach this union is yoga.

How can this union be achieved?

There are several ways. But let us start at the beginning—with our ideas of what constitutes an individual. If I were to start telling you things you did not know, you would have a choice: to believe or disbelieve me. Either way, you have only concretized your assumptions, whether positive or negative. This will only take you into flights of fanciful imagination. But the whole process of yoga is to take you, step by step, and stage by stage, *from the known into the unknown*. It is a hundred percent empirical science. It does not ask you to take anything on trust. It urges you to experiment every step of the way.

So, first let us look at what exactly you understand by the word "myself." Right now, in your understanding, this "you" is constituted by your body, your mind (which includes your thoughts and emotions), and your energies. Your energies may not be in your experience currently, but you know them by inference: if your body and mind function as they do, there must be some kind of energy empowering them. These three realities—body, mind, energy—are what you know. They are also what you can work with.

Yoga tells us that we are actually composed of five "sheaths," or layers or, more simply, bodies. As there is a medical physiology, there is a yogic one as well. It leads us from the gross to the subtlest levels of reality. Do you have to believe in it? No. But it is a useful place at which to start our exploration. Your fundamental area of work, however, is only with the realities that you are aware of.

The first sheath or layer to which yoga draws our attention is the physical body—the *annamayakosha,* or more literally, the food body. What you call the "body" right now is just an accumulated heap of food. It is the product of all the nourishment you have ingested over the years. That is how it gets its name.

The second layer is the *manomayakosha,* or the mental body. Today, doctors are talking a great deal about psychosomatic ailments. This means that what happens in the mind affects what happens in the body. This is because what you call "mind" is not just the brain. It is not located in any single part of the human anatomy. Instead, every cell has its own intelligence, so there is an entire mental body, an entire anatomy of the mind.

Whatever happens in the mental body happens in the physical body, and, in turn, whatever happens in the physical body happens in the mental body. Every fluctuation on the level of the mind has a chemical reaction, and every chemical reaction, in turn, generates a fluctuation on the level of the mind.

The physical and mental bodies are like your hardware and software. Hardware and software cannot do anything unless you plug into quality power. So, the third layer of the self is the *pranamayakosha,* or the energy body. If you keep your energy body in perfect balance, there will be no disease in your physical or mental bodies. Today there is scientific evidence to show that the impact of genetic memory on the human being is not absolute. Except the fundamental aspects of the DNA, everything can be changed, including the genetic trends of susceptibility to ailments. Infectious diseases happen because of external organisms, but chronic diseases are manufactured daily by human beings. When your energy body is in full vibrancy and proper balance, chronic diseases cannot exist in the body. I could introduce you to thousands of people who have gotten rid of their physical and psychological ailments just by doing certain simple yogic practices. These practices are not aimed at the disease. They are just aimed at bringing a certain harmony and vitality to the energy body.

These are the three dimensions of the self you are aware of right now: the physical, the mental, the energetic. They are essentially physical in nature, though each is more subtle than the preceding one. It is like a lightbulb, electricity, and light— all these are physical. One you can hold in your hand; the other you can feel; and the third takes a sensitive receptor, like the eye, to experience. But they are essentially physical, which is why you can experience them through your sense organs.

However, there is a fourth layer called the *vignanamayakosha,* or the etheric body. *Gnana* means "knowledge." *Vishesh gnana* means "extraordinary knowledge"—that which is beyond the sense perceptions. This is a transient state. It is neither physical nor non-physical. It is like a link between the two. It is not in your current level of experience, because your experience is limited to the five sense organs which cannot perceive the non-physical. Those who report near-death experiences are those who could have slipped accidentally into this state. Such an experience occurs when, for some reason, people's physical, mental, and energy bodies have become feeble. If you learn to find conscious access to this dimension, there will be a quantum leap in your ability to know the cosmic phenomenon.

There is also a fifth sheath, the *anandamayakosha,* which is beyond the physical entirely. *Ananda* means "bliss." It has nothing to do with the physical realms of life. A dimension that is beyond the physical cannot be described or even defined, so yoga talks about it only in terms of experience. When we are in touch with that aspect beyond the physical, we become blissful. It is not that a bubble of bliss lies within your physical structure. It is just that when you access this indefinable dimension, it produces an overwhelming experience of bliss.

But bliss is not a goal in itself. Once you touch this dimension of nonexistence, blissfulness is guaranteed. In this state, you are no more an issue in your own life. When you are no more an issue, you can fearlessly explore the beyond.

When you touch this dimension beyond definition, the impact of time and space is obliterated. This accounts for the many stories of yogis sitting unmoving for incredibly long periods of time. This is possible not because of physical endurance, but because in these states, they are not available to the process of time. They have touched a dimension beyond all the contradictions of here and there, now and then; a limitless ocean of emptiness where there is neither bondage nor freedom—an existence beyond existence.

Yoga does not ask you to work with anything other than what you know. It simply tells you that if the physical, mental, and energy bodies are perfectly aligned, you will find access to the bliss body. But your work, as we said before, is only with the first three bodies.

When it comes to external realities, each human being is differently capable. What one does, the other may not be able to do. But when it comes to inner realities, all of us are equally capable. There is no guarantee that you will be able to sing, dance, climb a mountain, or make money, merely because you want to. But making your inner life blissful is something that everyone is capable of. It *cannot* be denied to you, if you are willing. Once you master certain basic yogic technologies of inner well-being, your journey through life becomes absolutely effortless. You are able to express yourself at your fullest potential without any stress or strain. You can play with life whichever way you want, but life cannot leave a single scratch upon you.

∽

So, to experience well-being all you need is a certain mastery over these three dimensions of body, mind, and energy. Being successful in the world depends on your ability to harness these dimensions, according to the needs of your life situations and the activity you want to perform. But yoga is also the science of aligning these three dimensions so that you reach the ultimate state of ecstatic union with life itself.

How does one reach this ultimate union?

Yoga tells us there are a few fundamental ways. If you employ your physical body to reach this ultimate union, we call this *karma yoga*, or the yoga of action. If you employ your intelligence to reach your ultimate nature, we call this *gnana yoga*, the yoga of intelligence. If you employ your emotions to reach your ultimate nature, we call this *bhakti yoga*, the yoga of devotion. And if you use your energies to reach the supreme experience, we call this *kriya yoga*, the yoga of transforming energies.

Every human being is a unique combination of the same ingredients. All these aspects—karma, gnana, bhakti, kriya—have to function in an integrated way, if one wants to get anywhere. If these four dimensions—body, mind, emotion, energy—don't walk together, you will be one big mess.

Once it happened . . . Four men were walking in the forest. The first was a gnana yogi, the second was a bhakti yogi, the third was a karma yogi, and the fourth was a kriya yogi.

Usually, these four people can never be together. The gnana yogi has total disdain for every other type of yoga. His is the yoga of the intellect, and typically, an intellectual has complete disdain for everybody else, particularly these devotional types who look upward and chant God's name all the time. They look like a bunch of idiots to him.

But a bhakti yogi, a devotee, thinks all this gnana, karma, and kriya yoga is a waste of time. He pities the others who don't see that all you need to do is know that God exists, hold his hand, and walk in trust. All this mind-splitting philosophy, this bone-bending yoga is absurd to him.

Then there is the karma yogi, the man of action. He thinks all the other types are just plain lazy. Their lives are pure self-indulgence.

But the kriya yogi is the most disdainful of all. He laughs at everyone. Don't they know that existence is just energy? If you don't transform your energy, whether you long for God or for anything else, nothing is going to happen! There can be no transformation.

These four people customarily cannot get along. But today they happened to be walking together in the forest. Suddenly, a storm broke out. It grew fierce. The rain started pouring down relentlessly. Drenched to the skin, the four yogis started running, looking desperately for shelter.

The bhakti yogi, the devotion man, said, "There's an ancient temple in this direction. Let's go there." (As a devotee, he was particularly familiar with the geography of temples.)

They ran in that direction. They came to an ancient temple; all the walls had crumbled long ago; just the roof and four columns remained. They rushed into the temple—not out of any love for God, but just to escape the rain.

There was a deity in the center. They ran toward it. The rain started lashing from every direction. There was no other place to go, so they moved closer and closer. Finally, there was no alternative. They just sat down and embraced the idol.

The moment these four people hugged the idol, suddenly God appeared.

In all their minds the same question arose: why *now*? They wondered, "We expounded so many subtle and arcane philosophies, worshipped at every possible sacred shrine, great and small, selflessly served so many people, did so much body-breaking penance, but you never showed up. Now when we're just escaping the rain, you turn up. Why?"

God said, "At last you four idiots got together."

❧

Yoga is, quite simply, the science of bringing the four idiots together.

Right now, for most people, these four dimensions are aligned in different directions. Your mind is thinking one way; your emotions pull you another way; your physical body another way; your energy another way. This makes you a potential calamity, an accident waiting to happen. You are being hijacked—you are being pulled apart, in four different ways.

It is now time to plunge into the adventure of self-alignment, into the remarkable empirical system that is yoga—one that enables you to be both alchemist and experiment, subject and object at the same time.

And so, the next section of this book turns pragmatic. Having mapped the terrain, we now embark on a real journey, a conscious journey of self-discovery and self-reclamation. We will explore the nature and possibilities of the first three yogic layers, or sheaths—namely, body, mind (which includes thought and emotion), and energy. It will also introduce you to strategies by which you can turn each of these layers into a tool for transformation, an instrument of knowing.

The problem is that religious nuts around the world have exported everything that is beautiful about a human being to the other world. If you talk of love, they speak of divine love. If you talk of bliss, they speak of divine bliss. If you talk of peace, they speak of divine peace. We have forgotten that these are all *human* qualities. A human being is fully capable of joy, of love, of peace. Why do you want to export these to heaven?

There is so much talk of God and heaven mainly because human beings have not realized the immensity of being human. It is obvious that the very source of life is throbbing within you in some way. The source of your life is also the source of every other life and the source of all creation. This dimension of intelligence or consciousness exists in every one of us. The deliverance of every human being lies in finding access to this deathless dimension.

To be joyful and peaceful within yourself every moment of your life, to be able to perceive life beyond its physical limitations—these are not superhuman qualities. These are human possibilities.

Yoga is not about being superhuman; it is about realizing that being human is super.

PART TWO

A Note to the Reader

The next part of the book grows more specific, taking you deeper into an exploration of the three fundamental sheaths, or layers, of identity, that every human being is conscious of. Accordingly, it is divided into three sections: Body, Mind, and Energy.

Within each section, the book seeks to extend your ideas of what constitutes the physical, the psychological, and the *pranic* (or energetic). In the process, you may find some assumptions interrogated, some clichés punctured, some commonly used terms redefined, and some unusual perspectives explored.

But you are required to take nothing on faith. Yoga, as we have said before, asks you to experiment—and encourages you to do so fearlessly. And so, this section oscillates between information and suggested practice and self-observation exercises. It concretizes concepts and suggests ways to implement ideas. In the process, you can find out for yourself whether these concepts are workable, or if they are simply so much hot air.

What is the best way to approach this section? You may not feel inclined to implement each of the exercises offered in the "Sadhana" boxes. That is absolutely fine. The reason for offering you a range of practices and tips is so that you can zero in on any that appeal to you. These steps are simply intended to help you make the transition from the page to the business of daily living, to offer you the freedom to test every hypothesis in the laboratory of your own life. This section aims at turning you from a passive reader, an armchair yogi, into a dynamic participant in the magic of a life consciously lived, freely chosen.

It's time to roll up your preconceived notions and gear up for an uninhibited exploration of the incredible life that you are.

Body

The Ultimate Machine

The most intimate part of physical creation for all of us is our own bodies. The physical body is the first gift of which we are aware. It is also the ultimate machine. Every other machine on the planet has come out of this.

The yogic sciences, as explained above, do not speak of the mind or the soul. Everything is just a body—whether it is a food body, a mind body, an energy body, an etheric body, or a bliss body. There is a deep wisdom in this approach. It does not allow us to escape into deluded psychological states or into flights of metaphysical abstraction. It grounds us firmly in the tangible, even as it leads us into subtler realms of physicality and, gradually, into the beyond.

The physical body is designed and structured to function by itself without much of your intervention. You don't have to make the heart beat, the liver perform all its complex chemistry, or even try to breathe; everything that is needed for your physical existence to manifest itself is happening on its own.

The body is a pretty complete and self-contained instrument. If you are fascinated by machines, there isn't a better one! This is the most sophisticated piece of machinery on this planet—it embodies the highest level of mechanics, the highest level of electronics, the most sophisticated electrical circuitry you can imagine.

Let us say you eat a banana this afternoon. By evening, this banana has become *you*. According to Charles Darwin, it took millions of years to make a monkey into a human being, but in just a few hours you are capable of making a banana or a piece of bread into a human being! Obviously, *the very source of creation is functioning within you.*

There is an intelligence at work within you, way beyond your logical mind, which can transform a bit of food into the highest piece of technological excellence. If you could achieve that transformation consciously (instead of unconsciously), if you could bring even a drop of that intelligence into your daily life, you would live magically, not miserably.

It is because he experienced the source of creation throbbing within him that the twelfth-century Indian mystic Basavanna famously called the body a "moving" temple. "My legs are pillars," he says in one of the well-known verses of South Indian mystical literature, "the body the shrine / the head a cupola of gold . . ."

"Something there is that doesn't love a wall"

It takes a certain amount of awareness for a person to see the limitations of this fantastic machinery. As a machine, the body is actually faultless. The only problem is that it does not take you anywhere. It just springs out of the earth and falls back into the earth.

Isn't that enough?

If you look at it from the perspective of the body, it *is* quite enough. But somehow, a dimension beyond physicality has infused itself into this wonderful mechanism. This dimension is the very source of life. It is this dimension that truly makes us who we are.

Life is one thing, but the source of life is another. In every creature, in every plant, in every seed, this source of life is at work. In a human being, this source of life is even more magnificently obvious.

It is because of this that suddenly after a while, all the wonderful gifts that the body offers somehow seem to turn irrelevant and trivial. It is because of this that you and every other human being seem to live in a constant struggle between the physical and the dimension beyond the physical. Though you have the compulsiveness of the physical, you also have the consciousness of being more than just physical.

There are two basic forces within you. Most people see them as being in conflict. One is the instinct of self-preservation, which compels you to build walls around yourself to protect yourself. The other is the constant desire to expand, to become boundless. These two longings—to preserve and to expand—are *not* opposing forces, though they may seem to be. They are related to two different aspects of your life. One force helps you root yourself well on this planet; the other takes you beyond. Self-preservation needs to be limited to the physical body. If you have the necessary awareness to separate the two, there is no conflict. But if you are identified with the physical, then instead of working in collaboration, these two fundamental forces become a source of tension.

All of the "material-versus-spiritual" struggles of humanity spring from this ignorance. When you say "spirituality," you are talking about a dimension beyond the physical. The human desire to transcend the limitations of the physical is a completely natural one. To journey from the boundary-based individual body to the boundless source of creation—this is the very basis of the spiritual process.

The walls of self-preservation that you build for today are the walls of self-imprisonment for tomorrow. Boundaries that you establish in your life as a protection for yourself today will feel like constraints tomorrow. Robert Frost captured a deep truth when he wrote, "Something there is that doesn't love a wall."

Because your self-preservation instinct keeps telling you, "Unless you have walls you are not safe," unconsciously you keep building them. Later, you struggle with them. This is an endless cycle. But creation is not unwilling to open to you the doors to the beyond. It is not creation's unwillingness that you are struggling with. You are struggling with the walls of resistance that *you* have built around yourself.

That is why the yogic system does not talk about God. It does not talk about the soul or heaven. Such talk invariably makes people hallucinatory. Yoga talks only about the barriers that you have set up, because this resistance is all that needs to be attended to. The Creator is not looking for your attention. The ropes that bind you and the walls that block you—these are one hundred percent of your making. And these are all you need to unknot and dismantle. You have no work with existence. You only have work with the existence that *you* have created.

If I were to use an analogy, I would juxtapose gravity and grace. Gravity is related in a way to the fundamental instinct of self-preservation in a human being. We are rooted to the planet right now because of gravity. We have a body today only because of gravity. Gravity is trying to hold you down, whereas grace is a force that is trying to lift you up. If you are released from the physical forces of existence, then grace bursts forth in your life.

As gravity is active, grace too is constantly active. It is just that you have to make yourself available to it. With gravity you have no choice; you are available to it, anyway. If you are strongly identified with the physical, gravity is all that you will know. But with grace, you have to make yourself receptive. Whatever kind of spiritual practice you do, ultimately, you are just working toward making yourself available to grace.

When you are available to grace, suddenly, you seem to function like magic. Suppose you were the only one who could ride a bicycle, you would begin to seem magical to everyone else! It is the same with grace. Others might think you *are* magic, but you know you are just beginning to become receptive to a new dimension of life. This possibility is available to everybody.

Sadhana

You may have noticed this about yourself: when you are feeling pleasant, you want to expand; when you are fearful, you want to contract. Try this. Sit for a few minutes in front of a plant or tree. Remind yourself that you are inhaling what the tree is exhaling, and exhaling what the tree is inhaling. Even if you are not yet experientially aware of it, establish a psychological connection with the plant. You could repeat this several times a day. After a few days, you will start connecting with everything around you differently. You won't limit yourself to a tree.

Using this simple process, we at the Isha Yoga Center have unleashed an environmental initiative in the southern Indian state of Tamil Nadu, under which thirty million trees have been planted since 2004. We spent several years planting trees in people's minds, which is the most difficult terrain! Now transplanting those onto land happens that much more effortlessly.

Life Sense: Knowing Life
Beyond the Senses

How does the human body make sense of the world? What is its source of knowing?

The answer is obvious: through the five senses.

Whatever you know of the world or yourself is information you have gathered only through the five sense organs—by seeing, hearing, smelling, tasting, and touching. If these sense organs fold up, you would know neither the world nor your-self.

When you sleep every night, suddenly the people around you disappear, the world disappears, and even *you* disappear. You are still alive, everybody around you is alive, but in your experience everything evaporates, because these five sense organs have gone into "shutdown" mode.

The sense organs are limited. They can perceive only that which is physical. If your perception is limited to the five senses, naturally the scope of your life will be restricted to the physical. Additionally, the senses perceive everything only *in relation to* something else. If I touch a metal object and it feels cool to my fingers, it is simply because my body temperature is warmer. Suppose I lower my temperature and touch it, it would feel warm to me.

The sense perceptions are absolutely wonderful instruments for human survival. They are turned on at the moment of your birth because they are essential to your survival in the outside world. But if you are seeking something more than survival, they are not enough. They give you a distorted impression of reality because they are entirely relative in their perception.

If you are really interested in knowing life in all its depth and dimension, it is imperative that you look inward, not out. Why? Because the essential nature of life does not lie in the physical or psychological expression of body and mind, but in their source. However, looking inward doesn't happen easily. It takes work, because you don't yet have the perceptual mech-anisms to look within. The human predicament is just this: *the very seat of your experience is within you, but your per-ception is entirely outward bound.*

This is why there is such a big disconnect between within and without. You can see what is outside you, but you cannot see what is inside you. Even if someone whispers, you can hear it, but there is so much activity happening in the body that is beyond your ability to hear. If even an ant crawls upon your skin you can sense it right away, but there is so much blood flowing within you that you cannot feel. Your sense organs can only register external sensations of sight, sound, smell, taste, and touch. But the source of all experience is *within* you. An experience may be triggered by an external stimulus, but its origin is always internal—and there are times when the same experience can be generated even without an external trigger.

Yoga is fundamentally aimed at enhancing your experience beyond the five senses. There *is* a dimension beyond your five sense perceptions. You can call that dimension whatever you please. You can call it "self," if you choose. You can call it "divine," if you choose. You can term it "God," if you choose. The terminology is entirely up to you.

And even if you are not in quest of the divine or the self, enhancing your perception can play a vital role in assuring a fundamental level of well-being. Whatever you are— doctor, policeman, engineer, artist, homemaker, or student— fundamentally, it is your quality of perception that determines how effective and successful you are and how much you can do on this planet. The expansion of your perception beyond its present boundaries can achieve phenomenal results, bringing a completely new and seemingly magical dimension to your life.

The common questions are: "Is it very difficult to enhance my perception? Do I have to withdraw to a Himalayan cave to turn inward?"

Not at all. This possibility does not come from sitting somewhere on top of a mountain; it is within you. The only reason it has been inaccessible is that you are either busy or preoccupied with what is happening outside or far too engaged in your own psychological drama. It is just a lack of attention which has denied people the possibility of discovering what lies within.

Turning inward does not have anything to do with thoughts, ideas, opinions, or philosophies. It has nothing to do with the psychological activity of your mind. Enhancing your perception means enhancing your ability to receive life, just as it is. If you are willing to dedicate just a few minutes of your life to this every day, you would see the change. The simple process of paying a little bit of attention to your inner nature will transform the quality of your life in remarkable ways.

Sadhana

Start by paying attention to everything you think of as yourself just before you fall asleep: your thoughts, your emotions, your hair, your skin, your clothes, your makeup. Know that none of this is you. There is no need to make any conclusion about what "you" are or what "truth" is. Truth is not a conclusion. If you keep the false conclusions at bay, truth will dawn. It is like your experience of the night: the sun has not gone; it is just that the planet is looking the other way. You're thinking, reading, talking about the self, because you're too busy looking the other way! You haven't paid enough attention to know what the self really is. What is needed is not a conclusion, but a turnaround. If you manage to enter sleep with this awareness, it will be significant. Since there is no external interference in sleep, this will grow into a powerful experience. Over time, you will enter a dimension beyond all accumulations.

Listening to Life

There are several ways to attain a state of abiding joy and ultimate union. These are diverse, but it is important that they are all addressed in a balanced and integrated way. There is really no division or hierarchy between these varied approaches. Yoga is completely evenhanded: it employs *all the aspects* of who you are to take you to your ultimate destination.

The body constitutes a very large part of who you are in your present understanding. The science of using the body to hasten your evolutionary process is hatha yoga. *Ha* denotes the sun and *tha* denotes the moon. Hatha yoga is the science of bringing about a balance between these two dimensions within the human system.

The body has its own attitudes, its own resistance, its own temperament. Let us say you decide, "Starting tomorrow, I will get up at five in the morning and go for a walk." You set the alarm. The alarm rings. You begin to stir, but your body groans and says, "Shut up and sleep." That is often the way it is, isn't it? So, hatha yoga is a way of working with the body, a way of disciplining, purifying, and preparing it for higher levels of energy and for greater possibilities.

Hatha yoga is *not* exercise. It is, instead, about understanding the mechanics of the body, creating a certain atmosphere, and then using physical postures to channel or drive your energy in specific directions. This is the aim of the various *asanas,* or postures. That kind of posture that allows you to access your higher nature is a *yogasana*. It is the science of aligning your inner geometry with the cosmic geometry.

To put it in the simplest way, just by observing the way some people sit, you can almost know what is happening with them, if you have known them long enough. If you have observed yourself, when you are angry, you sit one way; if you are happy, you sit another way; if you are depressed, you sit another way. For every different level of consciousness, or psychological state, your body naturally tends to assume certain postures. The converse of this is the science of asanas. *If you consciously get your body into different postures, you can elevate your consciousness.*

The body can become a means for your spiritual growth or it can become a barrier. Let's suppose some part of your body—your hand, leg, or back, for instance—is in pain. When the pain is acute, it is hard to aspire to anything higher because that pain becomes dominant in your life. Right now if you have a backache, the biggest issue in the universe is your back. Other people may not understand that, but for you, that *is* the biggest issue. Even if God appears before you, you will plead for your backache to go away! You will not ask for anything else because the physical body has such power over you. When it doesn't function as it should, it can rob your life of every other aspiration. All your longings just disappear once the body is in pain. To experience pain and still look beyond it takes an enormous amount of strength, which most people do not possess.

There are countless people who have come out of spinal problems by doing simple asanas. Doctors had told them they would have to undergo surgery, but they were able to avoid it altogether. Your back can be restored to such an excellent condition that you never need to visit a chiropractor again. It is not only your spine that becomes flexible; *you* become flexible as well. Once you are flexible, you are willing to listen. It is not about hearing someone talk; you are willing to *listen to life*. Learning to listen is the essence of intelligent living.

Dedicating a certain amount of effort and time to see that the body does not become a barrier is important. A painful body can become an obstacle, and so can a compulsive body. Simple compulsions, whether of hunger or lust, can rule you so strongly that they will not allow you to look beyond the physical. It is easy to forget that the physical body is only *a part* of you; it is important that it does not become the whole of you. Asanas help level the physical body down to its natural place.

As you move into deeper dimensions of meditation, your energies will surge upward, opening up more profound dimensions of experience. It is very important, therefore, that the pipeline of the body is conducive. If it is blocked, it will not work. And so, preparing the body sufficiently before one goes into more intense forms of meditation is very important.

Hatha yoga ensures that the body takes the upsurge of energy smoothly and joyfully.

For a lot of people, spiritual growth happens very painfully because the necessary preparation has not taken place. Most human beings have unfortunately allowed themselves to be molded entirely by external situations. It is becoming a norm in the world that growth happens only painfully. It can also happen blissfully, but that is when both the body and mind have been prepared. Asanas can prepare you for growth and transformation by equipping you with a solid and stable foundation.

Today, the hatha yoga that people are learning is not the classical form in its full depth and magnitude. The "studio yoga" that you see today is largely the physical aspect of the science. Just teaching the physical aspect of yoga is like having a stillborn baby. It is not only inefficient; it is a tragedy. If you want a live process, it needs to be transmitted in a manner that is inclusive of other dimensions of yoga.

Hatha yoga does not mean standing on your head or holding your breath. It is the way that it is done that makes all the difference. There was a time when I personally taught hatha yoga as a two-day program. People would be overwhelmed with intensity at these programs; tears of ecstasy would flow, simply with the practice of asanas. Why doesn't this happen more often? Simply because hatha yoga is being imparted as an end unto itself, rather than as a preparatory system. Consequently, while the hatha yoga in the world today brings peace for a few and health for others, it is unfortunately a painful circus for many. This may be fine for someone whose aspiration is only peace and health. But you are looking at yoga as a means of transforming yourself into a receptive possibility beyond the five senses, the hatha yoga needs to be approached in its classical form.

Sadhana

Look around. Among your family, coworkers, and friends, can you see how everyone has different levels of perception? Just observe this closely. If you know a few people who seem to have a greater clarity of perception than others, watch how they conduct their body. They often have a certain poise without practice. But just a little practice can make an enormous difference. If you sit for just a few hours a day with your spine erect, you will see that it will have an unmistakable effect on your life. You will now begin to understand what I mean by the geometry of your existence. Just the way you hold your body determines almost everything about you.

Another way of listening to life is paying attention to it experientially, not intellectually or emotionally. Choose any one thing about yourself: your breath, your heartbeat, your pulse, your little finger. Just pay attention to it for eleven minutes at a time. Do this at least three times a day. Keep your attention on any sensation, but feel free to continue doing whatever you are doing. If you lose attention, it doesn't matter. Simply refocus your attention. This practice will allow you to move from mental alertness to awareness. You will find the quality of your life experience will begin to change.

Downloading the Cosmos

Until a few years ago in India, after every storm, you had to go up to your roof and adjust your TV antenna. Only if it was angled in a certain way did the world pour into your living room. Or else, as you were watching your favorite soap opera or cricket match, a blizzard would suddenly appear on your screen.

The body is like that antenna: if you hold it in the right position, it becomes receptive to all there is in existence. If you hold it another way, you will remain absolutely ignorant of everything beyond the five senses.

Here is another analogy: Your body is like a barometer. If you know how to read it, it can tell you everything about you and the world around you. The body never lies. So in yoga, we learn to trust the body. *We transform the physical body from a series of compulsions of flesh, blood, and hormones into a conscious process, a powerful instrument of perception and knowing.* If you know how to read the body, it can tell you your potential, your limitations, even your past, present, and future. That is why the fundamental yoga starts with the physical body.

It is as simple as this. The more you know about your telephone or any other gadget, the better you can use it. A few years ago, the cellphone companies conducted a survey, and found that ninety-seven percent of the people were using only seven percent of a phone's capabilities. I am not talking about the smartphone here, but the "dumb" one! Even with that simple gizmo, people were using *only seven percent*.

Now, as we have already said, this body of yours is the ultimate machine, the perfect state-of-the-art gadget. What percentage of *this* machine do you think you are employing?

Well below one percent! To conduct your life in the material world, to ensure your survival, you do not need even one percent of the body's capabilities. We are doing all kinds of trivial things with it because right now our whole perception of life is limited to the physical nature of existence. But your body is capable of perceiving the whole universe. If you prepare it properly, it can grasp everything in this existence, because all that happens to this existence is happening, in some way, to this body.

All physical creation is fundamentally a certain perfection of geometry. Without geometry, no physical form is possible. If we get the geometry of the human body right, it becomes capable of reflecting the larger geometry of the cosmos within, and making the cosmic available for our experience. In other words, the human body is capable of downloading the entire cosmos.

Sadhana

Sit in any comfortable posture, with your spine erect, and if necessary, supported. Remain still. Allow your attention to slowly grow still as well. Do this for five to seven minutes a day. You will notice that your breath will slow down.

What is the significance of slowing down the human breath? Is it just some respiratory yogic acrobatics? No, it is not. A human being breathes twelve to fifteen times per minute, normally. If your breath settles down to twelve, you will know the ways of the earth's atmosphere (i.e., you will become meteorologically sensitive). If it reduces to nine, you will know the language of the other creatures on this planet. If it reduces to six, you will know the very language of the earth. If it reduces to three, you will know the language of the source of creation. This is not about increasing your aerobic capacity. Nor is it about forcefully depriving yourself of breath. A combination of hatha yoga and an advanced yogic practice called the *kriya*, will gradually increase your lung capacity, but above all, will help you achieve a certain alignment, a certain ease, so that your system evolves to a state of stability where there is no static, no crackle; it just perceives everything.

INTENSITY OF INACTIVITY

Logically, somebody who never put effort into anything should be the master of effortlessness. But it is not so. If you want to know effortlessness, you need to know effort. When you reach the peak of effort, you become effortless. Only a person who knows what it is to work understands rest. Paradoxically, those who are always resting know no rest; they only sink into dullness and lethargy. This is the way of life.

For the Russian ballet dancer Nijinsky, his entire life was dance. There were moments when he would leap to heights that seemed humanly impossible. Even if one's muscles are at peak performance, there is still a limit to how high one can jump. But in some moments he would seem to transcend even that limit.

People often asked him, "How do you manage this?"

He said, "There is no way I can ever do it. When Nijinsky is not there, only then it happens."

When someone is constantly giving a hundred percent, a point comes when one surpasses all limits and reaches total effortlessness. Effortlessness does not mean becoming a couch potato. It means transcending the need for physical action. Only when you are able to stretch to your utmost and sustain the peak of effort do you reach this. There are some people nowadays, who declare that they would like to opt for Zen as a spiritual path because they think it means doing nothing! In fact, Zen involves tremendous activity because it is not divorced from life in any way. For example, a Zen monk may take weeks to simply arrange pebbles in a Zen garden. In performing such activity, you reach a state of non-doing, where you transcend the experience of being a doer. It is in such states that you have a taste of the beyond.

If you achieve such states through intense activity, as Nijinsky and many others have, those moments will always be cherished as magical. But if you arrive at the same state through the *intensity of inactivity*, then it is a yogic posture, and it is a state that can be sustained longer.

The very essence of *dhyana*, or meditativeness, is that you push yourself to the highest possible intensity where, after some time, there is no effort. Now meditation will not be an act, but a natural consequence of the intensity that has been achieved. You can simply be. It is in these absolutely non-compulsive states of existence that the necessary atmosphere is set for the blossoming of an individual into a cosmic possibility.

If we, as societies and individuals, continue to allow every moment to pass by without setting the atmosphere for such a flowering, we have squandered a tremendous possibility. There is so much infantile talk about heaven and its pleasures only because the immensity of being human has not been explored. If your humanity overflows, divinity will follow and serve you. It has no other choice.

Morsel of the Earth

Your physical body, as yoga reminds us, is annamayakosha, or a food body, just a heap of the nourishment you ingest. The food that you consume is, in turn, just the earth. You are a small outcrop of this planet prancing around and claiming to be an autonomous entity. But since you are a small extension of the earth, whatever happens to the planet happens to you too—in some subtle and sometimes not-so-subtle ways.

This planet is part of a larger body that we call the solar system. What happens to that system affects the planet. This solar system is part of a larger body we call the universe. Maybe it is beyond your perception right now, but because your physical form is just a fragment of the planet, everything that is happening to any part of the universe is also in some way happening to you!

As incredible as it sounds, if you maintain your physical body in a certain way, you will become aware of subtle changes that happen in the planet and the cosmos. Once you become sensitive to it, your whole body feels everything happening around you. If you spend more time and pay attention to the ways of the earth, this sensitivity will increase dramatically.

I lived on a farm for a few years. There was a man in the local village who was hard of hearing. His name was Chik-kegowda. Because he could barely hear, he could not respond to people, so they thought he was an idiot. He was rejected by the village and made an object of ridicule. I employed him as my man on the farm. He was a nice companion to have because I wasn't particularly interested in talking, and he could not talk because he could not hear. So, no problem! Those were the days before tractors; life on the farm was all about bullocks and ploughs. One day, suddenly, at four o'clock in the morning, I saw him preparing the plough.

I asked him, "What's happening?"

He said, "I am getting ready to plough, sir."

I said, "But what will you plough? There is no rain."

He said, "It will rain today."

I looked up. It was an absolutely clear sky. I said, "What nonsense! Where is the rain?"

He said, "No, sir, it *will* rain."

And it did.

I sat up for days and nights after this. Why couldn't I feel what this man could feel? I sat, holding my hand in different positions, trying to feel the moisture, the temperature, trying to read the sky. I read all kinds of books on meteorology, but it felt like I was up against a wall. But then, with careful observation of my own body and what was around me, I discovered the most fundamental mistake that most of us make: the fact that *we view the ingredients which constitute our body, like earth, water, air, and food, as commodities and not as an organic part of the life process.*

After persevering for about eighteen months, I understood. And now if I say it is going to rain, ninety-five percent of the time it will. This is not astrology or magic, but a surmise based on the minute observation of a completely different level of the human system and its ongoing transaction with the planet, the air, and everything around. If it is to rain today, some change *will* happen in your body. Most urban-dwellers cannot feel it, but many rural people all over the world do sense this. Most insects, birds, and animals can feel it. A tree for sure knows it.

Recognizing these small changes in the planetary system, the ancients tried to make use of them not just for their own well-being, but for transcendence. The magnetic equator of the planet flows through India. A few thousand years ago, yogis pinpointed the exact location of the magnetic equator and built a whole string of temples along this area for very specific reasons. One of the most famous temples is the South Indian temple of Chidambaram, which was set up for those who sought ultimate spiritual union. At the time of its construction, it was located exactly on the magnetic equator (which has since shifted).

Many spiritual seekers gathered in Chidambaram over the

centuries at those times when the planet was in a certain position. In this temple, a shrine was consecrated by Patanjali, the father of yoga, to *shoonya,* which literally translates into "emptiness" or "no-thing." This is not mere symbolism. At the magnetic equator there is no pull toward north or south; there is zero degree of magnetic play, and this promotes a certain balance and equanimity in the life of the spiritual seeker. This equanimity can be a powerful device to liberate oneself quite literally from the limitations of the physical world, which makes this region the ideal geographic location for a seeker. (It is important to remember that the magnetic equator is distinct from the geographic equator.)

The additional significance of Chidambaram is that it happens to be located on eleven degrees latitude. When it was built, there was a convergence of the magnetic equator with this latitude—a rare and important occurrence. What was the significance of this location? The tilt of the planet at this latitude impels centrifugal forces in a nearly vertical direction, which, in turn, pushes energy upward through the human physiological system. This means that the ascent of human energy—the aim of the spiritual journey—is actually assisted by nature. Since this was a great source of encouragement to seekers, this entire region was considered to be sacred. (It is not a coincidence that the Isha Yoga Center in South India is located bang on eleven degrees latitude.)

The kind of spiritual system described above makes use of natural phenomena to support human efforts at spiritual growth. Another system—of meditativeness, or inwardness—completely ignores the changes happening in creation and focuses solely on the inner journey. These are the two fundamental ways in which the spiritual journey can be approached: you can either go slowly, step-by-step, accepting all natural assistance available to you, or you can ignore all the steps and take the inward leap. The second entails a withdrawal from external life situations; the first makes involvement mandatory. Every human being is free to choose the path more suitable to his or her temperament. In the times in which we live, a balance between the two is usually best.

Sadhana

The body responds the moment it is in touch with the earth. That is why spiritual people in India walked barefoot and always sat on the ground in a posture that allowed for maximum area of contact with the earth. In this way, the body is given a strong experiential reminder that it is just a part of this earth. Never is the body allowed to forget its origins. When it is allowed to forget, it often starts making fanciful demands; when it is constantly reminded, it knows its place. This contact with the earth is a vital reconnection of the body with its physical source. This restores stability to the system and enhances the human capacity for rejuvenation greatly. This explains why there are so many people who claim that their lives have been magically transformed just by taking up a simple outdoor activity like gardening.

Today, the many artificial ways in which we distance ourselves from the earth—in the form of pavements and multistoried structures, or even the widespread trend of wearing high heels—involves an alienation of the part from the whole and suffocates the fundamental life process. This alienation manifests in large-scale autoimmune disorders and chronic allergic conditions.

If you tend to fall sick very easily, you could just try sleeping on the floor (or with minimal organic separation between yourself and the floor). You will see it will make a big difference. Also, try sitting closer to the ground. Additionally, if you can find a tree that looks lively to you, in terms of an abundance of fresh leaves or flowers, go spend some time around it. If possible, have your breakfast or lunch under that tree. As you sit under the tree, remind yourself: "This very earth is my body. I take this body from the earth and give it back to the earth. I consciously ask Mother Earth now to sustain me, hold me, keep me well." You will find your body's ability to recover is greatly enhanced.

Or if you have turned all your trees into furniture, collect some fresh soil and cover your feet and hands with it. Stay that way for twenty to thirty minutes. This could help your recovery significantly.

In Sync with the Sun

The *surya namaskar* is a familiar sequence of postures to many who have practiced or know something of yoga. Generally, people understand the surya namaskar as a physical exercise. Others view it with some suspicion as some form of sun worship. It is neither. Yes, it most definitely does strengthen your spine and muscles and more, but that is not the objective.

What then is the significance of what is often seen as a sun salutation?

Firstly, this is not a salutation at all. It literally means organizing the solar energies within you, based on the simple logic that all life on this Earth is solar-powered. The sun is the life source for this planet. In everything that you eat, drink, and breathe, there is an element of the sun. Only if you learn how to better "digest" the sun—internalize it, and integrate it into your system—do you truly benefit from this process.

Those who do surya namaskars regularly find that their batteries last longer, with less need for recharge or replenishment. Additionally, the surya namaskar aids the balance or reorganization of inner energies, in terms of right and left, or lunar and solar dimensions. This produces an innate physical and psychological equilibrium that can be an enormous asset in one's daily life.

As I mentioned before, when I was young, I had to be forcibly awakened every morning by my mother. But once I began yoga, my system came awake effortlessly at a certain hour every day. Life began to happen with that much more ease and equanimity.

The surya namaskar is essentially about building a dimension within you where your physical bodily cycles are in sync with the sun's cycles, which run about twelve and a quarter years. It is not by accident but by intent that it has been structured with twelve postures. If your system is in a certain level of vibrancy and readiness, and in a high state of receptivity, then naturally your cycle will be in sync with the solar cycle.

Young women have an advantage because they are also in sync with the lunar cycles. It is an advantage, but a lot of them treat it as a curse. It is a fantastic possibility that your body is both connected to the solar *and* the lunar cycles. Nature has granted this advantage to a woman because she has been entrusted with the responsibility of propagating the human race. So she has been given some extra privileges, which unfortunately have been perceived socially as disadvantages. People do not know how to handle the bonus energy generated at that time and hence treat it as a curse, and even a kind of madness. (The word "lunatic" is derived, as we know, from "lunar.")

The physical body is a fantastic stepping-stone for higher possibilities, but for most people it functions as a roadblock. The compulsions of the body do not allow them to go forward. Practicing surya namaskar maintains physical balance and receptivity, and is a means of taking the body to the edge, so that it is not a hurdle.

Between the menstrual cycle, which is the shortest cycle (a twenty-eight-day cycle), and the cycle of the sun, which is over twelve years, there are many other kinds of cycles. The word "cyclical" denotes repetition. It also means going round in circles and not getting anywhere. Repetition means, on some level, compulsion. Compulsiveness implies something that is not conducive for consciousness.

Anything that is physical, from the atomic to the cosmic, is cyclical. Either you ride the cycle or are crushed by it. Yogic practice is always aimed at enabling you to ride the cycle, so you have the right kind of foundation for consciousness.

It must be remembered that the repetitive nature of cyclical movements or systems, which we traditionally refer to as *samsara*, offers the necessary stability for the making of life. If everything was random, it would not be possible to house a steady life-making machine. For the solar system and for the individual, being rooted in cyclical nature gives a certain firmness and steadiness to life. The very nature of the physical world *is* cyclical.

But once life has reached the level of evolution that human beings have attained, it is natural to aspire not just to stability, but to transcendence. Now, it is left to individual human beings either to remain trapped in the cyclical, or to use these cycles for physical well-being, or finally to go beyond the cyclical entirely.

If you are compulsive, you will see that situations, experiences, thoughts, and emotions in your life will be in cycles. They keep coming back to you once every six or eighteen months, three years, or six years, depending on your degree of compulsiveness. If you just look back on your life, you will notice this. If they come once every twelve years, that means your system is in a high state of receptivity and balance.

The surya namaskar is an important process to enable that to happen. On a rudimentary level, it is a complete workout for the physical system—a comprehensive exercise form without any need for equipment. But above all, it is an important tool that empowers human beings to break free from the compulsive patterns of their lives.

There are variations of this practice, depending on an individual's aspirations. Someone who seeks muscular fitness can practice a basic process that is known as *surya shakti*. Through practice, if one attains a certain level of stability and mastery over the system, one could be introduced to a more powerful and spiritually significant process called the *surya kriya*. While the surya namaskar is about balancing the two dimensions of sun and moon (or masculine and feminine) within the human system, the surya kriya is about connecting these two fundamental divisions for further spiritual growth.

A LEGENDARY YOGI

Raghavendra Rao, the yoga teacher I met as a boy, led a life that would be considered superhuman by conventional standards. He was known as Malladihalli Swami because he hailed from the village of Malladihalli, which is in the southwestern Indian state of Karnataka.

He was known to do 1,008 surya namaskars a day. Later, after he was ninety years of age, he brought the number down to 108 (not because he wasn't capable, but because there was no time). That was his spiritual practice.

In addition to being a yoga master, he was a wonderful Ayurvedic doctor. He was one of the few *nadi vaidyas*—traditional physicians who diagnose your ailment by feeling your pulse. He would not only tell you what disease you had today, but could predict what ailment was likely to afflict you in the next ten to fifteen years, and would teach the requisite remedial practices. One day in a week, he would be available in his ashram as an Ayurvedic doctor. Wherever he was, he would travel back to the ashram on Sunday evening to be there on Monday morning. If he sat down at four o'clock in the morning, he was there right through the day till seven or eight o'clock in the evening. Volunteers would come in shifts to help him, but he himself sat through the whole day. For every patient who came, he had a joke to tell. People would forget they had come for treatment. It was less like a doctor-patient interaction and more of a festival!

This happened when he was about eighty-three years of age: One Sunday, late at night, he was at a railway station about seventy-five kilometers from his ashram. He was with two companions, and they discovered that there was a railway strike. This meant no trains and no other means of transport. His commitment to his work was such that he left his two companions on the platform and just ran seventy-five kilometers overnight on the railway tracks!

At four o'clock in the morning he was at the ashram, ready to treat his patients. People at the ashram did not even realize that he had come running. Only when his other two friends reached there did they tell the others what Swamiji had done! That is how incredibly he lived. He lived up to the age of a hundred and six and taught yoga until his dying day.

Elemental Mischief

Life is a game of just five ingredients. Even sambar requires more ingredients! But in yoga both the human body and the cosmos are based on the magic of only five elements—earth, water, fire, air, and ether. Such a staggeringly complex phenomenon and just five variables! Not surprisingly, those who attained self-realization have often termed life a cosmic joke.

Once, when I was driving after midnight, I approached a mountain. As I drove toward it, I saw that almost half the mountain was ablaze! I am not known to shy away from danger, so I continued to drive. But I was cautious, because I knew I was in a car full of flammable fuel and I had my little girl in the backseat. It was misty and the farther I drove up the mountain, the fire always seemed to be a little farther away. Then I realized that although all the terrain that I saw from down below looked like it was on fire, as I drove into it, there was nothing at all.

When I reached the actual site of the fire, I saw that a truck had broken down. The driver and a couple of others had built a small fire for themselves because of the cold. As the mist reached dew point, the million droplets in the air, each one acting as a prism, created such a phenomenal illusion that a little fire seemed like a major conflagration. From down below, it looked like the whole mountain was aflame! That incident left me astounded.

Creation is just like that, hugely magnified. Those who have looked within themselves closely and attentively realized there was no need to look at the macro version. The entire cosmos is just a magnified projection of a little occurrence happening within you—the play of five elements. This is all it takes to make a throbbing full-fledged human being!

Maybe your desire is individual or maybe it is universal. But whether you want to realize the full potential of this human mechanism or merge with the larger cosmic mechanism, you need a certain measure of mastery over these five elements. Without this you know neither the pleasure of being an individual nor the bliss of uniting with the cosmic.

Whether your physical body is a stepping-stone or a hurdle on your path to well-being, essentially depends on how you are able to manage these five. If they do not cooperate with each other, nothing significant ever happens to you. But with their cooperation, your life—from the basic to the highest aspects—suddenly becomes a tremendous possibility.

The body is like a doorway. If you are always facing closed doors, then for you a door means a deterrent. If doors are always opening up for you, then for you a door means a possibility. They say how long a minute is essentially depends on which side of the bathroom door you are! Those inside say, "Just a minute, I'm coming." That one minute, for the person outside, is an eternity!

Every spiritual practice in the world is related in some way with organizing these five elements. The most fundamental practice in the yogic system is *bhuta shuddhi*—the cleansing of the elements in the physical system so that they work in harmony. All yogic practices are essentially derived from the cleansing of these elements. The basis of individual existence is actually memory, which penetrates deep into these five elements. Cleansing the elements of the compulsive tendencies that percolate into the individual as a result of mental, genetic, evolutionary, and karmic memory, helps bring a sense of absolute harmony between the individual and the cosmos. (We will look at the role of memory at greater length in a later chapter.)

When you achieve a level of expertise in your yogic practice, you approach what is called *bhuta siddhi*, or mastery over the elements. With this mastery, life opens up its bounty to you. Health, well-being, clarity, enlightenment—none of these can be denied to you anymore.

So whether you experience life as a great possibility or a great barrier simply depends on the extent to which these five elements cooperate with you. Freedom and bondage—both are determined by these five elements. The very existence that traps you also sustains you. This is the paradox of the life process. Love and hate, freedom and entrapment, life and death are all encapsulated in each other. If they were separate, there would be no problem; you could deal with them. The problem is, they are inextricable. If you try to avoid death, you only end up avoiding life!

In ancient India, there were courtesans who were masters in the art of seduction. They wore elaborate jewelry that seemed impossible to remove. The whole body was covered in ornaments. If you had to take them off one by one, it would take a long time. The man, fired up by lust, would want to undress this woman, but it was in vain. She would go on encouraging him with more intoxicants—a little more, a little more, and a little more. As his vision grew blurry, his task grew even more difficult, and eventually, he would fall fast asleep, snoring. But there was just one pin; all it took was to pull this one pin, and everything would fall down. That trick only *she* knew.

Life is a bit like that. It is a complex web, but there is one simple pin. And that is your identity. The play of five elements is highly evolved and complicated, but the key to freedom is your limited persona. If you pull the plug, it just falls apart and you are free. If you know how to pull yourself out, life's complexity collapses and everything settles. The simplicity of perfect alignment with existence is suddenly yours.

Sadhana

The simplest thing that you can do to change the health and fundamental structure of your body is to treat the five elements with devotion and respect. Just try this. Every time you are consciously in touch with any of the elements (which you are every moment of your life), just make a conscious attempt to refer to it in terms of whatever you consider to be the ultimate or the loftiest ideal in your life, whether it is Shiva, Rama, Krishna, God, Allah (or even Marx!). You are a psychological being right now, and your mind is full of hierarchy. This process will settle the hierarchy. After some time, the word can fall away. But you instantly see the change as the number of truly conscious moments in your life increases. The air that you breathe, the food that you eat, the water that you drink, the land that you walk upon, and the very space that holds you—every one of them offers you a divine possibility.

ENSHRINING THE ELEMENTS

In southern India, five major temples were built for each of the five elements. These temples were created not for worship but to facilitate a specific type of spiritual practice.

To cleanse the water element you would go to a particular temple and do one kind of practice. To cleanse the element of air, you would go to another. In this manner, five wonderful temples were created for each of the elements, infused with the kind of energy that assisted a particular type of spiritual practice. Traditionally, seekers traveled from one temple to another, to be initiated into practices that enabled them to have mastery over the elements and to achieve healing, well-being, and even transcendence.

These five temples were built so that they functioned as one system. This was a phenomenal technology. Those who knew the appropriate spiritual practice could make use of it. Those who did not know the practice could benefit just by living in that region. The temples still exist, and even those who do not understand their energy significance marvel at these magnificent works of architecture.

When the Shit Hit the Ceiling

Once it happened . . . One day in court the emperor Akbar asked, "What do you think gives the most pleasure to a person?"

There was a chorus of responses. One courtier said, "Serving God is the greatest pleasure, Your Highness."

There are always all manner of sycophants around emperors. So someone else said, "Oh my lord, serving you is the greatest pleasure I can conceive of!"

A third courtier said, "Just gazing at your face is the ultimate joy!"

The hyperbole poured forth. Birbal, the wise, just sat there, bored.

Akbar asked, "Birbal, what makes you so silent? What is it that gives *you* the greatest pleasure?"

Birbal said, "Shitting."

Until then, Akbar was feeling great with all the fawning and adoration. Now he got mad. He said, "For uttering such an obscenity in court, you had better prove it. If you can't prove it, your life is at risk."

Birbal said, "Give me a fortnight, Your Highness. I'll prove it to you."

Akbar said, "Fine."

The next weekend, Birbal organized a hunting trip for Akbar into the forest, and made sure all the women in the palace also traveled on this expedition. He set up the camp in such a way that Akbar's tent was in the center. All around, he placed the families, women and children. He told the catering department to produce the best food. They produced the choicest delicacies and Akbar ate well. He was on a vacation, after all.

The next morning when he got up and came out, he saw that there was no toilet tent. He went back into his tent and walked up and down, but the pressure was building up. He tried to go into the forest, but Birbal had made sure the womenfolk were all over the place.

Pressure built up by the minute. It was about twelve noon, and Akbar couldn't bear it anymore. He was just about to burst. Birbal, who was watching this whole scene, kept walking around, muttering, "Toilet tent, where to put it, where to put it?" He was simply creating confusion and delaying matters a little longer.

The emperor was full of shit, and just when there was no more time left, they managed to set up the toilet tent. Akbar went inside and moaned with relief. Then Birbal, who was waiting for him outside the tent, asked, "Do you agree with me now?"

Akbar said, "It *is* the greatest pleasure."

Relief from something that you cannot hold within you is always the greatest pleasure, isn't it? Whatever that thing may be!

So, the body *can* become an issue. A big issue. A barrier between you and your enjoyment of life.

If you want to maintain the body in a certain way, it is important to pay attention to the various activities of the body, in relation to food, sleep, and sex. We will look at each of these in turn in the next few pages.

Sadhana

❈

It is important not to keep eating through the day. If you are below thirty years of age, three meals every day will fit well into your life. If you are over thirty years of age, it is best to reduce it to two meals per day. Our body and brain work at their best only when the stomach is empty. So be conscious of eating in such a way that within two and a half hours, your food moves out of the stomach, and within twelve to eighteen hours completely out of the system. With this simple awareness you will experience much more energy, agility, and alertness. These are the ingredients of a successful life, irrespective of what you choose to do with it.

Food as Fuel

Your physical body is just an accumulation of food. Yoga pays much attention to food because what kind of food you put into the system has a tremendous impact on the kind of body you have constructed. There is a whole yogic science behind what to eat, how to eat, and when to eat. What kind of stuff you put into it determines the quality of the body and how comfortable it is with itself.

Are you preparing this body to run as swiftly as a cheetah? Or are you preparing this body to carry two hundred pounds? Or are you preparing this body so that it becomes conducive for higher meditative possibilities? You need to eat the right kind of food depending on your inclination and what you want out of your life.

The way you eat not only decides your physical health, but the very way you think, feel, and experience life. Trying to eat intelligently means understanding what kind of fuel this body is designed for and accordingly supplying it, so that it functions at its best.

Let us say you bought a gasoline car, but pumped diesel into it. It might still move around, but it would not function at its optimal capacity, and its life span would also be substantially reduced. Similarly, if we do not understand what kind of fuel this body is designed for, if we just force whatever comes onto our plate into our systems, it will definitely not function at its optimum capacity and its longevity could be seriously compromised. The compatibility of the fuel and the machine is of great importance if you are seeking a certain caliber of service.

What kind of food is the human system really designed for?

If you eat certain foods, the body becomes happy. If you eat certain other foods, the body turns dull and lethargic, and your sleep quota increases. If you sleep for eight hours a day, and you live a hundred years, you have spent one third of your life sleeping! Another thirty to forty percent is spent on food, toilet, and other ablutions. There is very little time left for life!

You eat food for energy, but if you eat a big meal, do you feel energetic or lethargic? Depending upon the quality of the food that you eat, you first feel lethargy, and then slowly you start feeling energetic.

Why is this so?

One aspect is the fact that your system cannot digest cooked food as it is; it needs certain enzymes to do so. All the enzymes necessary for the digestive process are not present in the body alone; the food that you eat also contains these enzymes. When you cook the food, generally eighty to ninety percent of the enzymes are destroyed. So the body is struggling to reconstitute these destroyed enzymes. The enzymes that you destroy in cooking can never be totally re-constituted, so generally, for most human beings, about fifty percent of the food that they eat becomes waste.

Another aspect is the stress on the system. The body has to process all this food just to get a small quota of energy for its daily activity. If we ate foods with the necessary enzymes, the system would be functioning at a completely different level of efficiency and the conversion ratio of food to energy would be very different. Eating natural foods, in their uncooked condition, when the cells are still alive, will bring an enormous sense of health and vitality to the system.

One can easily experiment with this. Don't ask your doctor, your nutritionist, or your yoga teacher. When it comes to food, it is about the body. Ask the body what kind of food it is most comfortable with, not your tongue. The kind of food your body feels most comfortable with is always the ideal food to eat. You must learn to listen to your body. As your body awareness evolves, you will know exactly what a certain food will do to you. You do not even have to put it into your mouth. You can develop this kind of heightened sensitivity whereby just looking at or touching the food will be enough for you to know its potential impact on your system.

Sadhana

You can experiment: arrange the best possible meal for yourself, get angry with something, curse the whole world, and then eat it. You will see that day how food behaves within you. At the next meal, approach your food with the reverence that the life-making material deserves and eat it. You will now see how it will behave within you. (Of course, if you're sensible, you'll ignore the first and only do the second!)

Most people can bring down the quantum of food they are eating to a third and be much more energetic and not lose weight. It is just a question of how much receptivity you have created within yourself. Accordingly your body receives. If you can do the same amount of work, maintain all the bodily processes, with thirty percent of the food that you eat, that definitely means you are running a much more efficient machine.

IN A NUTSHELL

The pranic value of all seeds is tremendous, because they represent concentrated life. This is quite apart from their enormous nutritional value. What you call a nut is essentially just a seed, and a seed is a wonderful possibility. A seed is the future of a plant's life. A single seed is capable of making the entire Earth green. Consequently, consuming anything in seed form can greatly enhance human health on many levels.

As far as possible, soak the nuts that you intend to consume in water for six to eight hours, especially if they are dry nuts. All seeds have a certain natural chemical self-protection. Soaking in water will flush out these toxic substances and bring them to the surface, and these can be eliminated by peeling off the skin of the nut. Additionally, soaking them helps lower the concentrated protein content which sometimes makes them difficult to digest.

Hell's Kitchen

There is an ongoing debate between the proponents of vegetarianism and non-vegetarianism. I am often asked which is better.

Vegetarians are often inclined to act holier-than-thou, while non-vegetarians often claim they are more robust and fit for the world, given that they are willing to include all the species on the planet on their menu. Great philosophies have evolved based on food choices.

In yoga, there is absolutely nothing religious, philosophical, spiritual, or moral about the food that we eat. It is only a question of whether the food is compatible with the kind of body that we own.

This compatibility depends on various ends. If being big is your highest aspiration, then certain types of foods have to be consumed. If you want a body that supports a particular level of intelligence, or if you want a body with a certain level of alertness, awareness, and agility, other types of foods must be consumed. If you are not someone who will settle just for health and the pleasures of life, but want a body perceptive enough to download the cosmos, you will need to eat in a very different way. Depending on your aspiration, you will accordingly have to manage your diet. Or if your aspirations involve all these dimensions, you will have to find a suitable balance.

Keeping aside our personal goals and aspirations, what type of fuel is this body designed for? This is something to which all of us should first pay attention. Modifications, adjustments, and adaptations of diet should come later. If it is simply a question of basic survival, eat whatever you want. But once survival is taken care of and there is a choice, it is important that you eat consciously, and are led not by the compulsion of the tongue but by the essential design of your body.

In the animal kingdom, you can largely classify animals as herbivores and carnivores—those that eat vegetable matter and those that consume meat or prey upon other animals. Between these two categories of creatures, there are fundamental differences in the design and construction of their physical systems. Since our focus is food, let us explore the digestive systems of each. The whole alimentary canal is a digestive tract from the lip to the anal outlet. If you travel down this tube, you will find some very fundamental differences between herbivores and carnivores. Consider a few significant ones.

For one, you will find that carnivores are capable of only a cutting action in their jaws, but the herbivores are capable of both cutting and grinding actions. We human beings have both cutting and grinding actions.

What is the reason for this design difference?

Suppose you take a bit of uncooked rice and place it in your mouth for a minute or more, you will notice that it turns sweet. This sweetness is happening because right there in your mouth carbohydrates are getting converted into sugar (an essential part of the digestive process) by an enzyme called "ptyalin," which is in your saliva. Ptyalin is present in the saliva of all herbivores, but not in carnivores. So carnivores just have to cut their food into smaller pieces and swallow it, while herbivores have to chew their food. Mastication involves grinding and then thoroughly mixing the food with the saliva; hence the design modification in the jaw.

If mastication happens properly, close to fifty percent of your digestive process would be finished in the mouth. In other words, the stomach region is expecting partially digested food to efficiently complete the process. In modern life, people are in such a hurry that we gulp our rush-hour lunches without the food being properly masticated.

The stomach is burdened not only with undigested food, but also with partially destroyed food. Today's kitchens have largely become places where food is efficiently destroyed. Food that is nutritious and full of life is systematically degraded through the cooking process, which depletes its nutritional value and largely obliterates its pranic value (its capacity to be spiritually supportive).

Next, if you look at the length of the alimentary canal, for herbivores it is generally about five to six times the length of their bodies. In carnivores, it ranges from two to three times the length of their bodies. To put it simply, carnivores have distinctly shorter alimentary canals than herbivores, and this difference clearly indicates what type of food each species is supposed to consume.

If you eat raw meat, it takes between seventy to seventy-two hours to pass through your system; cooked meat takes fifty to fifty-two hours; cooked vegetables twenty-four to thirty hours; uncooked vegetables twelve to fifteen hours; fruits one and a half to three hours.

If you keep raw meat outside for seventy to seventy-two hours, putrefaction sets in—one small piece of meat can evict you from your home! Putrefaction occurs very rapidly in the summertime, when the temperature and moisture are conducive. Your stomach is always a tropical place, and if meat stays there for up to seventy-two hours, the level of putrefaction is very high. This essentially means there is excessive bacterial activity, and your body must expend a lot of energy to contain the bacterial level, so that it does not cross the line that separates health from illness.

If you visit a friend who is sick in the hospital, you would surely not take him a pizza or a steak. You are most likely to take him fruit. If you happen to be in the wild, what would be the first thing you would eat? Definitely fruit. (You remember even Adam ate an apple, although we know what trouble that got him into!) Then would come roots, the killing of an animal, cooking, and raising crops. Fruit is the most easily digestible food and all human beings know this instinctively.

Most carnivorous animals do not eat every day—definitely not three times a day! They know the food they eat moves very slowly through their tracts. A tiger is said to eat once every six to eight days. He is agile and prowls when he is hungry, eats a hefty meal of fifty-five pounds of meat at once, and then generally sleeps or ambles around lazily. A cobra eats sixty percent of its own body weight in a single meal, and eats only once every twelve to fifteen days. The pygmies from the central African region used to hunt elephants, eat their organs and meat raw, and drink the blood fresh. They say they would sleep after this kind of meal for over forty hours at a stretch. But as lifestyles change and grow more urban and sedentary, it is clear that human beings cannot maintain such a mode of life. You certainly cannot afford this sort of lifestyle. You have to eat every day and rest at specific times because your alimentary canal is similar to that of the herbivores.

THE PROTEIN DEBATE

There is much emphasis laid nowadays on eating protein. It is important to understand that only three percent of our body is composed of protein and excess protein consumption can cause cancer. Meat runs high in protein. A very small portion of the meat that one consumes can fulfill the human protein requirement. The remaining portion, which travels very slowly through the alimentary canal, leads to a variety of problems such as excessive bacterial activity, enhanced sleep quota, increased inertia levels in the body, and decreased cellular regeneration. All of this, in turn, manifests as a drop in one's sensitivity of perception. It is in this context that meat has been regarded as spiritually unsupportive, because the spiritual process is essentially about enhancing one's perception beyond the limitations of the physical.

Digestion Drama

Another aspect of digestion is that to digest a certain kind of food the human system produces alkalis, and to digest another kind of food it generates acid. If you consume a jumble of foods, then the stomach grows confused and produces both acids and alkalis, which neutralize each other and make the digestive juices lose their edge. Hence the food remains in the stomach longer than required, and weakens our ability to rejuvenate on the cellular level.

It also causes what we refer to as *tamas,* or inertia, in the energy system, which over a period of time will alter the very quality of who you are and impair the quality of who you could be. Traditionally, in southern India, people took care never to mix certain foods. But today, food is no more about the well-being of the body, but a social affair. People eat out at buffets and the variety and number of dishes served is considered more important than nourishing the health and life of the body.

The question is not about what not to eat, but about how much of what to eat. It is not a moral issue; it is a question of life sense. As you battle city life, you need an agile and working mind, and physical and mental balance. And some of you even have spiritual aspirations—even if it is only every once in a while! So, every individual must arrive at his or her own balance of diet, not by taking vows, but by observation and awareness.

It is important not to turn into a food freak. Food should never become an all-consuming affair. Every creature on the planet knows what to eat and what not to. What is the human problem then? The human problem is not enough attention, but too much information.

The yogic science works essentially with the interiority of the human being. Out of its profound understanding of the science of the human mechanism, this science later branched out into various systems. One such outcome was the system of Ayurveda, which is growing increasingly popular once again in modern times. The word *ayur* means "life span" and the word *veda* means "science" or "knowledge." So, Ayurveda is the science of extending the human life span. It is a system that uses external plant life and earth elements to promote health and to correct systemic irregularities. Knowledge systems like these were intended to assist those who are incapable of doing the necessary yogic practice to achieve the same ends.

Sadhana

The consumption of a spoonful of clarified butter (ghee in India) on a daily basis a few minutes before a meal does wonders for the digestive system. If you eat clarified butter with sugar, as in sweets, it is digested and turns into fat. But clarified butter without sugar can cleanse, heal, and lubricate the alimentary canal. Additionally, the cleansing of the colon will immediately manifest as a certain glow and aliveness in your skin. Even those who prefer not to consume dairy products could experiment with this because clarified butter passes through the system largely without getting digested.

EVOLUTIONARY CODE

If you must eat non-vegetarian food, the best would be fish. Firstly, it is easily digestible with very high nutritional values. Secondly, it leaves the least amount of its imprint upon you.

What is meant by this?

Our bodies—all that we eat, excrete, and what eventually gets cremated or buried—is just earth. The software within your system determines that if you eat a fruit it is transformed into the human body, and not into a monkey or a mouse. The efficiency of your system obliterates the other software that transformed soil into a fruit and arrives at a new software that will make a fruit into a human form. For more evolved creatures, particularly mammals, their software is more distinct and individuated. This makes it harder for your code-breaking system to erase the software of the creature that you consume and to overwrite it with a new software.

Among the animals, fish, being one of the earlier forms of life upon this planet, have the easiest software code for our system to break and integrate into ourselves. Animals that have more intelligence, particularly those that are capable of a variety of emotions (such as cows or dogs), will retain their own memory systems. In other words, we are incapable of completely integrating more evolved, intelligent, and emotionally endowed creatures into our systems.

In earlier times, in communities that were more in tune with the earth, people could hunt and eat animals and work out the consequences through enormous amounts of physical activity. But given the largely sedentary lives people lead nowadays, the acidity produced by such a diet could contribute greatly to the unexplained levels of stress that are being widely experienced today. Additionally, large animals, particularly cows, are aware of their impending slaughter well before it happens. Consequently, they experience high stress levels, which generate a tremendous amount of acidic content in their systems. This, in turn, has its own adverse impact on those who later consume the meat.

Gastronomic Sense

If you observe the natural cycle of the body, you will find that there is something called a *mandala*. A mandala is a cycle of forty to forty-eight days that the human system goes through. In every cycle, there will be three days on which your body does not need food.

If you are conscious of how your body functions, you will become aware that on a particular day the body does not require food. Without effort, you can go without food on that day. Even dogs and cats have this awareness; on a particular day they often choose not to eat.

The day the system says "no food" is a cleanup day. Since most people are not aware of which day their body should go without food, the day of Ekadashi was fixed in the Indian calendar. Ekadashi is the eleventh day of the lunar segment and recurs every fourteen days. It is traditionally regarded as the day to fast. If some people are unable to go without food because their activity levels demand it, or if they do not have the appropriate spiritual practice to support it, they can opt to go on a fruit diet.

If you force yourself to fast without preparing your body and mind sufficiently, you will only cause damage to your health. But if your body, mind, and energy are properly prepared with the necessary practices, then fasting can be of much benefit to you.

People who are constantly on nicotine and caffeine will find that fasting can become very difficult. So before fasting, prepare the body by consuming the right kind of nourishment, particularly high-water-content foods like fruits and vegetables. It may not be a good thing for everybody to fast, but it has many benefits if it is done with proper understanding.

The entire aim and endeavor of yoga is to open up the cocoon of the physical body to the larger sensory body where you experience everything as a part of you. Fasting is an extension of this logic: it is a way of nourishing yourself without any active ingestion. It may be done as a detoxification process nowadays, but this is the internal rationale. This is why every spiritual tradition in the world has fixed a certain period of fasting for its adherents. In the yogic tradition, the fasting period was fixed according to the lunar cycle. This is because your ability to assimilate energy from water, air, and sunlight is greater on certain days of the lunar cycle. In some religions, the fasting period was fixed in peak summer when the consumption of water and sun by the human system would naturally be high.

My great-grandmother, a wonderful old woman, often considered eccentric by those who didn't know any better, would frequently give away her food to ants and sparrows. Tears of bliss would be streaming down her face as she did this. People around her kept saying, "Why don't *you* eat, old woman?" She'd simply reply, "I am full." But all those advisers died a long time before she did. She lived on and died at the incredible age of a hundred and thirteen!

My mother used to do this as well: every day before she ate her breakfast, she would take one handful of it and go looking for ants to feed. Only then would she eat. This has been a tradition among the womenfolk in many families. An ant is the smallest living entity you can see around you, the most inconsequential organism you can think of. So, for that very reason, you feed it first. You make an offering not to the gods, or other celestial creatures, but to the smallest creature you know. This planet belongs as much to them as it belongs to you. You understand that every creature on this planet has the same right to live as you have. This awareness can help create a conducive atmosphere, mentally and physically, for consciousness to grow.

Just a simple act like this loosens you from your identification with the physical body. As you become less of a body, your awareness of the other dimensions of who you are naturally becomes enhanced. When you are very hungry all your body wants to do is eat. Just wait for two minutes; you will find that it will make a big difference. When you are very hungry, you *are* the body. Give it a little space and suddenly you are not just a body.

Gautama the Buddha went to the extent of saying, "When you are badly in need of food, if you give away your food to somebody else, you will become stronger." I am not going that far with you; I am only saying, just wait a few minutes! It will definitely leave you stronger.

If you are very compulsive about food, it is good to miss one meal consciously. Try doing this: on a day when you are particularly hungry and some of your favorite dishes are being cooked, try skipping a meal. This is not to torture yourself; this is just to become free from the torture chamber that your body can very easily become.

What kind of food you eat, how much you eat, how you eat, turning it from a compulsive pattern into a conscious process: this is the essence of fasting.

Sadhana

⎯⎯⎯◆⎯⎯⎯

Just experiment. Start with twenty-five percent natural, uncooked, or live food—fruit or vegetables—today, and slowly push it up to a hundred percent in about four or five days. Stay there for a day or two, and again cut it down by ten percent and in another five days you will reach fifty percent raw food, fifty percent cooked food. This is ideal for most people, who wish to be active for sixteen to eighteen hours a day.

Remember, if you eat cooked food, it may take you fifteen minutes to eat a meal. If you eat raw food, you take a little more time to eat the same quantum of food, because you have to chew a little more. But the nature of the body is such that after fifteen minutes the body will tell you that your meal is over. So people tend to eat much less and lose weight. All it takes is being a little more conscious of how much you are eating.

Restlessness to Restfulness

The fact that you sleep at night makes some difference between your mornings and evenings. What is making the difference is the level of relaxation that sleep brings. If you could remain relaxed while performing all the activity of the day, you would be about the same in the evening, in terms of energy and enthusiasm, as you were in the morning.

If you wake up fresh, that is a good beginning, but slowly through the day, as your relaxation levels come down, you gradually start feeling stressed. Stress is *not* because of work— this is important to remember. Everybody thinks their job is stressful. No job is stressful. There are many jobs that could present challenging situations. There could be nasty bosses, insecure colleagues, emergency rooms, impossible deadlines—or you might even find yourself in the middle of a war zone! But these are not *inherently* stressful. It is our compulsive reaction to the situations in which we are placed that causes stress. Stress is a certain level of internal friction. One can easily lubricate the inner mechanism with some amount of inner work and awareness. So, it is your inability to handle your own system that is stressing you out. On some level, you do not know how to handle your body, mind, and emotions; that is the problem.

How then do you keep your system free of stress so that you remain in the same level of enthusiasm, relaxation, and happiness, whether it is morning or evening?

An average person's pulse rate on an empty stomach would be in the seventies or even eighties. For a person doing the right type of meditative practice, you will find that the pulse rate would range between the thirties and forties. Even after a good lunch it would stay in the fifties. This is just one parameter that indicates the level of restfulness that your body is experiencing moment to moment. Restfulness essentially defines the replenishing and rejuvenating capability of the body.

You cannot slow down your system at the cost of activity. What is necessary is to keep your system in such a way that activity does not take its toll upon it. Maybe physically you get exhausted, but it need not stress you in any way. If you are capable of being vibrantly active and still relaxed, then it is worthwhile. If you start certain simple practices of yoga, in three to four months' time, your pulse rate will drop at least eight to twenty counts very easily. That means the body is running so much more efficiently and at a relaxed pace.

What the body needs is not sleep but restfulness. If you keep the body very relaxed through the day, your sleep quota will go down naturally. If your work and taking a walk or exercising are also relaxation for you, your sleep quota will drop even further.

Right now, people want to do everything the hard way. I see

people walking in the park in a state of tension. Whether you walk or jog, why can't it be done easily, joyfully? This exercise may be causing more harm to you than well-being because you are going at it as if you're going into battle!

Don't battle with life. You are not anti-life; you *are* life. Just get in tune with it and you will see that you will pass through it easily. Keeping yourself fit and well is not a battle. Do some activity that you enjoy: play a game, swim, walk, run. If you don't like to do anything except eat cheesecake all day, then you have a problem! Otherwise, there is no incompatibility between being active and relaxed at the same time.

How much sleep does your body need? It depends on the level of physical activity you are engaged in. There is no need to fix the quota of either food or sleep. To program the calories you must consume and the number of hours you must sleep is a foolish way to handle life. Let the body decide how much it should eat today, not you. Today your activity levels are low, so you eat less. Tomorrow your activity is high, so you eat more. Similarly with sleep: when you feel sufficiently relaxed you come awake. The moment the body is rested it will wake up—whether it be at three or four or eight o'clock. When it comes to food and sleep, your body is the best judge.

If the body is at a certain level of alertness and awareness you will see that once it is well rested, it will awaken—that is, if it is eager to come to life. If it is somehow trying to use the bed as a grave, then it is a problem. Keep the body in such a way that it is not longing to avoid or escape life. Maintain it in such a way that it is longing to come awake.

Sadhana

If you sleep without a pillow or with a very low pillow, which doesn't allow the spine to get pinched, the neuronal regeneration of the brain and the cellular regeneration of the neurological system will be much better. If you sleep without a pillow, it is best to lie on your back in a supine position, rather than on your side. Lying in this position is referred to in yoga as *shavasana:* it enhances the purification and rejuvenation of the body, promotes the free flow of movement in the energy system, bringing relaxation and vitality. But there is no reason to get dogmatic about this. (At least in your sleep, don't take a position!)

Carnal to Cosmic

Existence is a dance between the unmanifest and the manifest. The moment there is a manifestation, there is duality: light and darkness, male and female, birth and death, and so on. Though unity is the basic fabric of creation, duality brings texture, design, and color to life. All the various manifestations that you see as life today are fundamentally rooted in duality. Because there are two, there are many. If there were only one, there would be no existence. Once there are two, the game of life begins.

Once duality begins, sex begins. What we call sex is just two parts of this duality striving to become one. In the process of these dualities meeting, there are also certain functions that Nature wants to fulfill, like procreation and the survival of the species. All duality is striving for unity because what was once one has manifested itself as two; now there is a perpetual longing to become one.

This longing to become one finds expression in many ways. When you are young and your intelligence is hijacked by your hormones, sex will be the way. When you are middle-aged and your intelligence is hijacked by your emotions, love is the way. When you are old and bereft of hormonal mischief, prayer is the way. But irrespective of age, when you transcend all this and seek the same union on a much higher level of awareness, then yoga is the way.

If you are seeking oneness with the body, you need to remember that physical bodies will always remain two, no matter what you do. For a few moments, a sense of unity will happen, and then people fall apart. If divorce does not do it, death will. It is bound to happen.

Sex is just two opposites making an attempt to become one. Your individuality means not only false boundaries that you have set up in your mental framework in the form of your preferences and dislikes, tastes and opinions. It also means you are trapped within the boundaries of your own physical body. You may not be consciously aware, but the life within you is longing to break these boundaries. When you want to break your mental boundaries you may long to have a serious conversation or read a book, drink alcohol, take a drug, or do something freaky. To break your physical boundaries you may want to pierce yourself, get a tattoo, dye your hair, or go the old-fashioned way of sex.

The intention of sex is great, but the method is hopeless.

Pleasure is involved, so it drives two people toward each other, but oneness comes only momentarily. So you try to meet in other areas of emotion and intellect. People are always trying to find common ground: "We like the same ice cream, both of us play videogames, share the same zodiac sign, and like the same TV shows . . ." But unless you understand that you can never become one, you will not learn to enjoy the opposite.

These two energies, which in the human race we call "masculine" and "feminine," are always trying to come together. At the same time, except for this longing to be together, they are opposites. They are lovers and enemies at the same time. If they look for similarities, there seems to be little common ground, but the attraction of the opposite is always there.

A lot of people cannot face the basic physical act as it is, so they have invented all kinds of decorations around it to make it beautiful. You always add emotion to it, because without emotion it would seem ugly. In some way you are trying to cloud your vision of reality with lots of decorations.

Sex is natural; it is there in the body. Sexuality is something you invented; it is psychological. If sex is in the body, it is fine, it is beautiful. The moment it enters your mind, it becomes a perversion. It has no business with your mind. Sex is a small aspect of you, but today it has become huge. For many, it has become life itself.

If you look at modern societies, I would say probably ninety percent of human energy is being spent either pursuing or avoiding sex. Sex is just nature's trick to reproduce. If this attraction of opposites did not exist, the species would become extinct. But now we have made such a distinction between man and woman, almost as if they are two separate species. No other creature on the planet has the kind of problems with sex that humans have. With animals, the urge is present in their body at certain times; otherwise they are free from it. With humans it is on their minds all the time.

One reason this has happened is that in the past, many religions went about denying a simple physical process to the extent of making it sinful. Because we could not even accept the biology of a human being, instead of looking beyond the limitations of the biological process, we tried to deny it. If we had no problem with biology, we would not make a distinction between who was who. Everybody would be known for what they are worth; whether somebody is male or female would be irrelevant. The whole exploitation of women starts once you cannot accept the fundamental differences between a man and a woman.

You do not have to make biology sacred, nor do you have to make it filthy. It is the instrument of life. Because of it you exist. If you know how to live it without elevating it or making it ugly, it has a beauty of its own.

The sensuousness that you experience in life is a chemical invitation for something that is not you to become a part of you. This is Nature's way of instigating you toward a union, or yoga. Though sensuousness is celebratory in its nature, it is discriminatory too. When two individuals are in a passionate meeting, the rest of the world is excluded, or even obliterated. If the celebration has to last, your sensuousness or your passion has to become all-inclusive. If you are in a state of all-inclusive passion, we call this yoga. So, *denial is not the answer. Expansion is the only answer.*

And if you have not known the sensuousness of the life-giving breath that is on every moment of your life, how can you even begin to know any other kind? Experiencing the orgasmic nature of the breathing process is called *ana pana sati yoga*, the yoga of incoming and outgoing breath. *Ana pana* literally means "in" and "out." *Sati* means "female consort." So, the reference here is clearly to orgasmic union. And so, ana pana sati yoga is a process that initiates you into a conscious and profound involvement with your breath, and shows you how the simple incoming and outgoing breath can become a source of nameless ecstasies.

Sadhana

The higher possibilities of life are housed in the human body. The physical body is a platform for all possibilities from the gross to the sacred. You can perform simple acts of eating, sleeping, and sex as acts of grossness, or you can bring a certain dimension of sanctity to all these aspects. This sanctity can be achieved by bringing subtler thought, emotion, and intention into these acts. Above all, remember that the grossness and sanctity of something is largely decided by your unwillingness and unconsciousness, or your willingness and consciousness. Every breath, every step, every simple act, thought, and emotion can acquire the stance of the sacred if conducted recognizing the sanctity of the other involved—whether a person or a foodstuff or an object that you use.

Of all the loving acts that two human beings are capable of, the simple act of holding hands can often become the most intimate. Why is this so? Basically, because the nature of the hands and feet is such that the energy system finds expression in these two parts of the body in a very singular way. Two palms coming together have far more intimacy than the contact between any other parts of the body.

You can try this with yourself. You don't even need a partner. When you put your hands together, the two energy dimensions within you (right-left, masculine-feminine, solar-lunar, yin-yang, etc.) are linked in a certain way, and you begin to experience a sense of unity within yourself. This is the logic of the traditional Indian *namaskar*. It is a means of harmonizing the system.

So, the simplest way to experience a state of union is to try this simple namaskar yoga. Put your hands together, and pay loving attention to any object you use or consume, or any form of life that you encounter. When you bring this sense of awareness into every simple act, your experience of life will never be the same again. There is even a possibility that if you put your hands together, you could unite the world!

Hormonal Hijack

I was once asked, "Isn't it strange that people are more obsessed with sex than any other physical urge?" Nothing strange about it. It is just the hormonal hijack we talked about earlier. In any case, sex is not the most powerful urge. Hunger is.

Most of the time, thinking about sex is just compulsive behavior. When you were a child, it did not matter what reproductive organs someone had. The moment the hormones started playing within you, you could not think of the world beyond that. And you will see that after a certain age, when the play of hormones subsides, once again it will not matter. You will look back and not believe you were the one obsessing about it.

There is nothing wrong with the body; it is just limited. Nothing wrong with being limited either. If you go by the way of the body, some pleasure may come to you. It is not a crime to want to be limited, but you will live an unfulfilled life.

Let us say tomorrow I grant you a boon and all the women or men in the world are lusting after you. You will find that you are still not satisfied. A little bit of pleasure and pain will happen, but you will only live within the sphere of the body. The body knows only survival and procreation. And it is walking straight to the grave every moment, nowhere else.

Your body is just a loan from this planet. What you call "death" is just Mother Earth reclaiming the loan that she offered to you. All life on this planet is just a recycle of the Earth. You may think right now that you are going to your office, home, or football match, but as far as your body is concerned, it is going, moment by moment, straight toward the grave. Right now, you may have forgotten, but slowly, as time passes, it will become more apparent that this is the nature of the body. If all that you have known is the body—and anyway you are going to lose it—anxiety and fear will be your constant companions.

People are even beginning to think that fear is a natural part of their existence. No. Fear is a result of the incompleteness of your existence. If you have not explored life in its magnitude and multidimensionality, but have limited yourself to the physical body, fear is a natural consequence.

Ever heard of George Best? He was one of the greatest footballers of his time in England. He was determined to make the most of his life in the way he knew best. The media described him as having every popular film star and fashion model on his arm at some time or the other. But by the time he reached the age of thirty-five, he was a broken, miserable, frustrated man; by the age of fifty-nine, he was dead. Death is not the issue, but the way you live *is* the issue. George Best supposedly had it all but he lived a terrible life.

This is because the way of the physical is circumscribed. The body has only so much of a role to play in your life. If you try to stretch it to all of your life, you will suffer because you are trying to create a falsehood. Life has a million ingenious ways to bend you, break you, knead you, and grind you.

Nothing wrong with your hormones, but once you live a compulsive life, you are living the life of a slave. Everything may be going on fine with your life—your business, family, relationships—but slowly, as different kinds of compulsions take over, you grow more and more miserable. There is something within you that is unwilling to be a slave. For many, the pursuit of wealth and physical well-being drives them to increasingly desperate actions. If you look under the veneer of civilization you will uncover the most abominable forms of abuse. We are not even sparing our own children. These are the consequences of not attending to all the dimensions of being human, and limiting ourselves to the narrow realm of the physical.

Today, in attempting to fetishize the body, people are creating untold suffering. You cannot think of a better arrangement materially: in terms of healthcare, insurance, cars. You have more comforts and conveniences than any previous generation. But people are suffering immensely. In affluent societies almost every fifth person is on some kind of medication just to maintain mental balance. When you have to take a tablet every day to remain sane, this is not joyfulness. You are on the verge of breaking down because you have made a small aspect of your life the whole of your life.

MORTALITY AND PROFUNDITY

Only when you recognize your mortal nature do you want to know what more there is to life. It is then that the spiritual process opens up.

Once it happened . . . Two men over eighty years of age met. One recognized the other and said, "Did you fight in World War II?"

The other man said, "Yes."

The first asked him where, and with which battalion. The other man told him.

The first exclaimed, "Oh, my God! Don't you recognize me? We were in the same foxhole!"

Oh, they hit it off! They talked and talked. All that they had actually seen was about forty minutes of an intense combat situation. But they talked about every bullet that went by, *zing*, *zing*, just missing them by inches. They spoke for over four hours about those forty minutes.

When they had exhausted everything that they could say about that time, one asked the other, "What have you been doing since the war?"

"Oh, for the past sixty years, I've just been a salesman."

Those forty minutes had come to define their lives because their mortality was dangling in front of them at every moment. In battle they had forged a bond that was profound. Beyond that, this man's life could be summed up in a single sentence: he was just a salesman.

You discover an indescribable profundity within yourself when you realize your mortal nature. If you have not realized your eternal nature you must at least realize your mortal nature. Death is not the end of life. Death is simply the end of the body. If you have lived with a very deep identification with the physical, the more you will struggle with death, because death marks the end of the body. Only when you confront your mortality—the potential but inevitable termination of your physical form—does the longing to go beyond become genuine.

Mind

Miracle or Mess?

Once it happened . . . A man wished to acquire supernatural powers. He went from one guru to another, desperately in search of instruction. He eventually found his way to a remote hermitage in the Himalayan wilderness.

The guru of the ashram divined the purpose of his quest and tried to dissuade him. "What will you do with these powers? So what if you learn to walk upon the water? After three days, a boat will be better! Don't waste your life on these irrelevant pursuits. Let me teach you meditation instead." The master made many attempts to dissuade him, but the man was adamant.

The guru finally said, "Well, if you're so determined, take a dip in the river tomorrow morning at four o'clock and come to me. I will initiate you into the secrets of the supernatural."

The man was excited. He took a pre-dawn dip in a freezing Himalayan river, turned half blue, and came and sat expectantly before the master.

The guru said, "See, this is very simple. I have a secret mantra. If you utter it three times over for the next forty days, all the supernatural powers will be yours."

He then revealed the mantra:

Asatoma sadgamaya.

From ignorance, lead me to truth.

The guru said, "You have to repeat this sacred mantra three times a day for the next forty days and the entire realm of the supernatural will be yours. But when uttering the mantra, just don't think of monkeys."

The man was incredulous at the simplicity of the practice. "Is that all?" he asked joyfully. "May I leave now?"

The guru said, "By all means. Please go and return in forty days."

The man left in a state of great excitement. "The fool of a guru revealed all his secrets to me without even charging a fee!" he thought. "And he is telling me not to think of monkeys. Why would I think of monkeys? Ridiculous!"

He came down the mountainside and reached the banks of the river Ganga. He took a dip in the holy river and sat down to begin his practice. But no sooner had he uttered the word "asatoma"—and monkeys! Each time a monkey popped into his head, he took another dip in the river. He attempted the mantra in various yogic postures. But each time he uttered the very first syllable, monkeys would appear. In hordes. In one week of intense practice, there was no need of a mantra anymore. It was a universe full of monkeys—a simian nightmare. Harassed by these countless monkeys, unable to do a thing, the man went all the way back to the guru and said, "I don't want your damn supernatural powers. Relieve me of these monkeys first!"

If you tell yourself you don't want to think a certain thought, that is precisely the first thing your mind will produce! That is the nature of the human mind.

In recent times, much scientific research has been conducted on the activity of the brain. If you look at the way neurons fire in the brain, there is a tremendous cohesiveness in this activity. It is this cohesiveness that translates into the efficient functioning of the body. A billion sophisticated activities are being performed in your body right now because of the highly coordinated and complex dance of neurons.

But the mind, in most people's experience, has unfortunately become a circus. A circus is actually a very coordinated activity, deliberately made to look like a mess. Even the clown in the circus is a gymnast. He may play the buffoon, but he is hugely talented and skillful in what he does. The metaphor of the clown sums up the experience of most people when it comes to their mental activity.

How did the mind, that amazing gymnast, become a clown? How did it turn from a source of magic to such a mess? Why has this miraculous instrument become such a misery-manufacturing machine?

As noted earlier, every human being is essentially seeking pleasantness, within and without. When it comes to the outside, there are a million ingredients, and nobody has complete mastery over them. When it comes to the inner situation, however, there is only one ingredient: *you*. You can be the sole architect and creator of your inner life. But you don't know how. That is the rub. If you were in charge, for sure you would not manufacture misery for yourself. A fundamental freedom you have is to *think* whatever you want. What then stops you from thinking pleasant thoughts?

The problem is just this: the fact that your mind is not taking instructions from you. Imagine a Paleolithic caveman punching a computer keyboard. What's going to come up on screen will look like a series of obscenities!

The system of yoga is a technology to create *a distinction between you and your mind*. There is a space between you and what you have gathered in terms of body and mind. Becoming conscious of this space is your first and only step to freedom. It is the accumulated physiological and psychological content that causes the cyclical patterns in your life and even beyond. If you can be constantly conscious of this space between you and the body-mind, you have opened up a dimension of limitless possibility.

There are only two forms of suffering in this world: physical and mental. Once this distance becomes a constant factor in your experience, you have reached the end of suffering. With the elimination of the fear of suffering, you can walk life full stride, unafraid to explore all that life has to offer. Your ability to use this immensely sophisticated body-mind phenomenon can be raised to a completely new dimension of experience and utility as you stand outside of them. This sounds paradoxical, but it is true. As the experience of space grows, the mind is no more a mess. It is a great symphony, a tremendous possibility that can take you to great heights.

Yoga is a journey toward a reality in which you experience the ultimate nature of existence as *borderless unity*. This experience is possible only if you maintain that space between you and your body-mind. It is important to remember that this borderless unity is an experience, not an idea, philosophy, or concept. If you vouch for the oneness of the universe as an intellectual theory, this may make you popular at a dinner party or win you applause at a seminar. You may even get a Nobel Prize. But it does not serve any other purpose. The *experience* of borderless unity, on the other hand, can deliver you to another dimension altogether—a dimension of love and blissfulness, a dimension far beyond the cerebral.

It can actually be damaging to an individual to see everything as one, intellectually. People often profess all kinds of fancy philosophical theories about becoming one with the cosmos, about loving the entire world, until life teaches them a good lesson. When it comes to money, the boundary between self and other is abundantly clear. At such times, there is no question of you and me being one!

Once it happened . . . Shankaran Pillai went to a Vedanta class. Vedanta is the school of Indian metaphysics that speaks of the non-duality of the self and the divine. The teacher, a learned philosopher, was in full swing: "You are not just this or that; you are everywhere. There is nothing like 'yours' and 'mine'; everything is you, everything is yours. In essence, everything is one. What you see, hear, smell, taste, touch is not reality; it is all *maya,* all illusion."

This unbeatable Vedanta rhetoric was buzzing in Shankaran Pillai's head. He went home and slept on it. He woke in the morning, totally fired up. Usually he loved to sleep, but because of this Vedanta, he sprang out of bed. The first thoughts in his mind were, "There is nothing which is not mine. Everything is mine; everything is me. All that is in this world is me, and everything is maya."

You know, whatever the philosophy may be, hunger happens at regular intervals. So Shankaran Pillai went to his favorite restaurant, ordered a big breakfast, and devoured it, saying to himself, "The food is me; the one who serves is also me; the one who eats is also me." Vedanta!

He finished his breakfast. When he was in such a high state of Vedanta, mundane issues like paying the bill did not occur to him. He rose and started walking out. When everything is yours, how can there be a bill?

As he passed the cash counter, the owner happened to turn away to attend to some other chore. Shankaran Pillai saw a huge heap of currency in the till. Immediately, Vedanta told him, "Everything is yours; you cannot differentiate between this and that." So because his pockets were quite empty, he put his hand into the box, took some cash, stuffed it in his pocket, and sauntered out of the restaurant. He was not out to rob anybody; he was just practicing Vedanta.

Suddenly a few people from the restaurant ran up and caught him. Shankaran Pillai said, "Who are you trying to catch? You are the catcher and the caught; what you catch is you; the one that catches is also you. When there is no such thing as you and me, who can I pay?"

The owner was bewildered! Only one thing was clear to him: "My cash is in your pocket." But here was Shankaran Pillai saying, "The one who catches is also me, the one who is caught is also me." The owner didn't know how to deal with this kind of customer. At his wits' end, he took Shankaran Pillai to court.

There, Shankaran Pillai continued his Vedanta. The judge

tried in many ways to make him understand that he had committed a theft, but to no avail. Then the judge gave up and said, "Okay, ten lashes on the backside."

First lash . . . Shankaran Pillai screamed.

The judge said, "Don't worry. It's all maya anyway. There is no such thing as pain and pleasure. Everything is maya."

Second lash . . . Shankaran Pillai shouted, "Enough!"

The judge said, "The one who lashes is you, the one who is lashed is also you."

Third lash . . . Shankaran Pillai hollered, "Stop stop!"

"There is no such thing as starting and stopping. It is all maya."

It was like this all the way to ten lashes. But before the ten were done, Vedanta had been cleaned right out of Shankaran Pillai.

An intellectual understanding that is not backed by experiential knowledge can lead to mind games and deceptive states. But if oneness becomes an experiential reality, it will not produce an immature action. It will produce a tremendous experience of life that will leave you transformed forever.

Universality is not an idea; it is an existential truth. It is individuality that is an idea. Yoga is simply *chitta vritti nirodha*. That means, if the activity of your mind ceases and you are still alert, you are in yoga.

But don't try to forcibly stop the mental activity because you will go insane. With your mind, all the three pedals are throttles; there are no brakes and no clutch. Have you noticed this? Whatever pedal you hit, the mind only accelerates its speed. But if you don't pay any attention to it, thoughts will slowly subside, leaving you in a rich and vibrant silence.

Sadhana

——∞——

Remind yourself at least once an hour that everything you're carrying—your handbag, your money, your relationships, the heaviness in your heart and body—are things that you've accumulated over a period of time. If you become more and more conscious of this fundamental fact even as a process of dis-identification grows within you—balanced by a deep sense of involvement in everything around you—you will move from the misery and madness of the human mind toward meditativeness.

Thinking Yourself Out of Life

It is only because you exist that you can generate a thought. But your thought process has become so compulsive that your focus has shifted from the existential to the psychological. This has happened to such an extent that you have begun to believe that you exist because you think! The foundations of Western philosophy actually rest on the famous axiom by the seventeenth-century French philosopher René Descartes: "I think, therefore I am."

It is time to restate a fundamental fact: *you are, therefore you may think.* This has nothing to do with any philosophy, Eastern or Western. It is a simple existential reality.

You can "be," and still choose to think or not think. The most beautiful moments in your life—what you might consider moments of bliss, joy, ecstasy, or utter peace—were moments when you were not thinking about anything at all. You were just *being*. Even without your thoughts, existence *is*.

What are thoughts really? Just information that you have gathered and recycled. Are you really capable of thinking of anything other than what has been accumulated by your mind? All the human mind is doing is recycling old data.

So I ask: Do you want to be a living being or a thinking being? Right now, ninety percent of the time, you are only thinking about life, not living it. Have you come into this world to experience life or to think about it? Your mental process is a very small happening compared to the life process, but right now it has become far more important. It is time for humanity to shift the significance to the life process once again. The need is an urgent one. Our lives depend on it.

Once it happened . . . (This is almost certainly an apocryphal tale, but that doesn't matter; it smells true.) Aristotle, the father of modern logic, the intellectual giant of ancient Greece, was walking on the beach. A glorious sunset was before him, but he had no time for such petty occurrences. He was thinking seriously about some great problem of existence. For the intellectual mind, existence is always a problem, and Aristotle was out to solve it. Lost in solemn thought, he paced up and down the beach.

There was another man on the beach who was doing something very intensely—so intensely that after a while even Aristotle noticed him. Those who are immersed in their own psychological realities usually end up ignoring life around them. They seldom have the eyes to look at a flower, a sunset, a child, or a smiling face. And if it is an unsmiling face, they have no inclination to make it smile; they have no such small duties or minor cares in the world! They are too busy cracking the great puzzles of existence.

But this man's intensity was such that even Aristotle could not ignore him. On close observation he noticed that this man kept going to the ocean and returning, with great single-mindedness of purpose. Aristotle paused in his reflections to inquire, "What exactly are you up to?"

The man said, "Please don't disturb me, I am doing something very important." He continued with his work with furious intensity.

Aristotle's curiosity was piqued. He asked again, "But what are you doing?"

The man said, "Don't disturb me. It is very important."

Aristotle said, "What *is* this important thing?"

The man showed him a little hole he had dug in the sand, and said, "I am emptying the ocean into this hole." He had a tablespoon in his hand.

Aristotle looked at this and laughed. Now, Aristotle is the kind who can spend a whole year without a single chuckle. It takes a heart to laugh. The intellect cannot laugh; it can only dissect.

But even Aristotle laughed at this and said, "This is ridiculous! You must be insane. Do you know how vast this ocean is? How can you ever empty this ocean into this little hole? And above all, with a tablespoon? At least if you had a bucket, you might have stood some chance! Please give this up. This is utter madness."

The man looked at Aristotle, threw the spoon down, and said, "My job is already done."

Aristotle said, "What do you mean? Forget about the

ocean being empty; even the hole is not full. How is your job done?"

The other man stood up and said, "I am trying to empty the ocean into this hole with a tablespoon. You are telling me it is madness. But what are *you* trying to do? Do you know how vast this existence is? It can contain a billion oceans like this and more, and you are trying to empty it into the small hole of your head—and with what? With tablespoons called thoughts! Please give it up. It's utterly ridiculous."

The other man was Heraclitus, the other great Greek phi-losopher. In a flash, he showed Aristotle what a crippled exis-tence he was leading by attempting to extend his logic to every aspect of life.

If you want to know the experiential dimensions of life, you will never know them with the petty process of thought. Even if you have the brain of an Einstein, your thought pro-cess is still outclassed because thought cannot be bigger than life. Thought can only be logical, functioning between two polarities. If you want to know life in its immensity, you need something more than the intellect.

This is the fundamental choice you have: either you learn to live with creation, or you manufacture your own creation in your head.

Which option do you want to exercise?

The planet is spinning on time: not a small event. All the galaxies are managing fine; the whole cosmos is doing great. But you have one nasty little thought crawling through your head, and it is a bad day! The problem is you are living in a psychological space that bears no connection with reality. And you are insecure, because it can collapse at any moment.

In the vastness and grandeur of cosmic space, if you look at yourself in perspective, you are less than a speck of dust. But you think *your* thought—which is less than a speck within you—should determine the nature of existence! You have lost your perspective of life: that is the basic problem.

You have heard of the "Buddha." His name was Siddhartha Gautama, and he *became* a Buddha. But Gautama was not the only Buddha. A human being who has transcended his intellect, the discriminatory and logical dimensions of his life, is a Buddha. Human beings have invented millions of ways to suffer. For all this the manufacturing unit is just in your mind. Once you are no longer identified with your mind, you are free to experience life beyond limitations. Being a Buddha means that you have become a witness to your own intellect.

The essence of yoga, as we have said before, is just this—to arrive at that moment where there is a clear space between you and your mind. Once this happens, a life of heightened clarity, perception, and freedom has begun. This is the birth of freedom.

LIMITS OF LOGIC

Without logical thinking, you couldn't survive on this planet. But at the same time, too much logic is suicide. Let us say you wake up tomorrow morning and start thinking a hundred percent logically. Do not think about the sunrise, the birds in the sky, your child's face, the flowers blooming in your garden. Just think logically.

Now, you have to get up, go to the toilet, brush your teeth, eat, work, eat, work, eat, sleep. Again, tomorrow morning the same thing. For the next thirty, forty, or fifty years, you have to do the same thing. If you think a hundred percent logically, there is no reason for you to be alive!

One day in New York City, a man was walking home, late from work. Suddenly he had a romantic idea. He went to the florist, bought a huge bunch of red roses, went home, and knocked on the door. His wife opened the door.

She looked at him and started hollering. "Today has been a terrible day. The faucet has been leaking, the basement is flooded, the children had a food fight, and I had to clean the whole place, the dog has been sick, my mother is not well, and you have the cheek to come home *drunk*!"

So if you think a hundred percent logically, there is really no possibility of life! Moments of extreme logic are moments of suicide. Only if you know when logic should be used and when it's necessary to go beyond it, will your life be beautiful.

Sadhana

You could try this simple practice. Set your tap in such a way that only five to ten drops fall per minute. See if you can observe each drop—how it forms, how it falls, how it splashes on the ground. Do this for fifteen to twenty minutes a day. You will gradually become conscious of many things around and within you that you are completely unaware of right now. This simple exercise can initiate a process of sensitization and clarity and accomplish much more than you can possibly imagine. In this simple process, you are actually exploring one limb of yoga referred to as *dharana*, which means "that which flows." It is not the water we are referring to here. It is your attention, and, in turn, your consciousness. The attempt is to make your attention flow and connect with its object—in this case, water. This is not an exercise in observation or appreciation. It is an exercise in attention—in turning what is sporadic and intermittent into a flow. (In the larger scheme of things, the water and you are already one. Your individuality is only your idea.)

The Grime of Identity

The intellect is like a scalpel. Its function is to slice through reality and enable you to discern one thing from another. If a knife has to cut through anything effortlessly, it is important that the substance it encounters does not stick to it. A sticky knife is obviously an ineffective implement.

Suppose you use a knife to cut a cake today; tomorrow you cut meat; and the day after tomorrow you cut fruit. If all these residues were to stick to the knife, it would turn over time into a useless instrument. You've probably experienced this already: if you cut mangoes or apples after cutting an onion, everything tastes like onion! Such a knife becomes more of a hindrance than a help. In other words, once your intellect gets identified with something, it gets chained to the identifications, and leaves you with a completely distorted experience of the world.

Once it happened . . . For political reasons, Akbar, the great emperor, was separated in his infancy from his mother. Another woman who had a child of her own was brought in to nurse him. This woman breastfed Akbar, and was later offered a reward for her services. Her boy, who was still a child, slightly older than Akbar, was allotted a few villages and was made a small ruler. Many years later, Akbar was crowned emperor. But this boy, who lacked the intelligence and capability required of a ruler, squandered all his resources, lost all that was given to him, and grew impoverished.

One day, when he was about thirty-two years of age, a grand idea occurred to him. He thought, "Since the emperor and I drank the same mother's milk, we are brothers. And since I was born first, I am the elder brother!"

With this idea planted firmly in his head, he went to Akbar and told him the same story. "See, we are brothers, and I am elder to you. But look at my sorry state: I am poor, you are an emperor! How can you leave me like this?"

Akbar was deeply moved. He welcomed him, set him up in the palace, and treated him like a king. The man was not accustomed to the ways of the court, and committed many stupid blunders. But the generous Akbar kept saying, "He is my elder brother. We have drunk the milk of the same mother." He introduced him to everybody as his elder brother.

This was the state of affairs for some time. Then it was time for the man to return to his village for some work. Akbar said, "My brother, you lost those villages given to you. I shall give you five new villages to rule—a small kingdom of your own."

The man said, "But I see that you have become this successful because there are lots of smart people around you. I don't have anybody to advise me, and that is why I'm lost. If only I had good advisers and ministers, I would also have built a major empire. Above all, you have Birbal! He's so smart. If only I had somebody like him I would also be a great emperor."

The large-hearted Akbar said, "If you wish, you may take Birbal with you."

He summoned Birbal and ordered him, "You must go with my elder brother."

Birbal said, "Your Highness, your elder brother deserves someone better than me. Why not *my* elder brother? I could send him instead."

Akbar thought that was a great idea because he did not relish the prospect of losing Birbal. Delighted, he said, "Summon him immediately."

The next day this man was to leave for his new kingdom, and a grand farewell was organized in court. There was a mood of anticipation in the air, as everyone waited for Birbal to arrive with his elder brother.

Finally, Birbal entered with a bull in tow.

"What is *this*?" Akbar asked.

Birbal said, "This is my elder brother."

Akbar was furious. "Are you trying to insult me and my brother?"

"No, my lord," said Birbal. "He *is* my elder brother. Both of us drank milk from the same mother."

Once your intellect—or *buddhi,* as it is termed in the yogic taxonomy—gets identified with something, you function within the realm of this identity. Whatever you are identified with, all your thoughts and emotions spring from that identity. Right now suppose you identify yourself as a man, all your thoughts and emotions flow from that identification. If you identify yourself with your nationality or religion, they will flow from those identifications. Whatever your thoughts and emotions, these identifications are a certain level of prejudice. In fact, your mind is itself a certain kind of prejudice. Why? Because it functions from limited data and is fronted by an essentially discriminatory intellect. So, your mind, which should have been a ladder to the divine, is stumbling through endless mediocrity and, on some occasions, has become a straight stairway to hell.

The identity around which the intellect functions is called *ahankara.* To continue with the earlier knife analogy, the hand that wields the knife is identity. Or in other words, it is your identity that manages and determines your intellect. When you use a knife, it is important not just to have a sharp blade, but a stable hand to hold it. Without a stable hand you can end up cutting yourself in a million different ways. Most of the suffering human beings undergo is not because of external situations. What is inflicted on them from the outside is minimal; the rest is all self-help!

Once you are identified with something that you are not, the mind is an express train that cannot be stopped. If you put the mind on full steam and want to apply the brakes, it will not work. But if you are able to disentangle yourself from everything that you are not—if you dis-identify, as it were—you will see that the mind turns just blank and empty. When you want to use it, you can; at other times, it will simply be empty, devoid of all psychological clutter. That is how it should be. But right now, you are identified with so many labels, and at the same time you are trying to stop your mind: this will simply not work.

Irrespective of what you think you are, when death confronts you, every identification falls away. If human beings learned to drop these voluntarily, life would be blissful. If you do not encumber your intellect with any identifications— body, gender, family, qualifications, society, race, caste, creed, community, nation, even species—you travel naturally toward your ultimate nature. If not, death will demolish it all anyway. You need have no doubt about that!

If you employ your intelligence and make an attempt to reach your ultimate nature, this is called gnana yoga, or the yoga of knowing. Gnana yogis cannot afford to identify themselves with anything. If they do, that is the end of their journey. But unfortunately, what has happened to gnana yoga, at least in India, is that its proponents entertain several beliefs. "I am the Universal Soul, the Absolute, the Supreme Being"— they know it all, from the arrangement of the cosmos to the shape and size of the soul! They have read all these things in a book. This is *not* gnana yoga. Any information you have about that which is not a living experience for you, is irrelevant. Maybe it is very holy irrelevance, but it does not liberate you; it only entangles you!

On a certain day, a bull was grazing on a field. He went deep into the forest, and after weeks of grazing on lush grass, became nice and fat. A lion, who was past his prime and having difficulty hunting his prey, saw this nice fat bull, pounced on him, killed him, and ate him up. His stomach became full. Then with great satisfaction, he roared. A few hunters were passing by. They heard the roar, tracked him down, and shot him dead.

Moral of the story: when you are so full of bull you should not open your mouth.

Very few people have the necessary intellect to pursue gnana yoga one hundred percent. Most need a huge amount of preparation. There is an entire yogic process to make your intellect so razor-sharp that it does not stick to anything. But it is very time-consuming because the mind is a tricky customer; it is capable of creating a million illusions. Gnana yoga as a part of your spiritual pursuit is a workable proposition; as an exclusive path, it is only for a very rare few.

Sadhana

Just sit alone for an hour. No reading, no television, no phone, no communication, nothing. Just see in the course of this hour what thoughts dominate your mind—whether it is food, sex, your car, your furniture, your jewelry, or anything else. If you find yourself thinking recurrently about people or things, your identification is essentially with your body. If your thoughts are about what you would like to do in the world, your identification is essentially with your mind. Everything else is just a complex set of offshoots of these two aspects. This is not a value judgment. It is just a way of knowing what stage of life you're at. How quickly you want to evolve depends on your own choices.

Soak the Intellect in Awareness

In the yogic system of classification, the mind has sixteen dimensions. These sixteen fall into four categories. There is the *discerning*, or discriminatory, dimension of the mind or the intellect (*buddhi*); the *accumulative* dimension of the mind, or memory (*manas*), which gathers information; and what is called *awareness* (*chitta*), which is beyond both intellect and memory. The fourth dimension, *ahankara*, we discussed earlier—the aspect of the mind from which you derive your sense of identity.

The first dimension—the intellect, buddhi—is crucial for your survival. You are able to discern a person from a tree only because your intellect is functional. You know that you must walk through the door, not through the wall, only because your intellect is functional. Without this dimension of discernment, you would not know how to survive on this planet. On more complex and sophisticated levels, the intellect has contributed immeasurably to human culture and civilization.

The problem of our times, however, is that the intellect has taken on a disproportionately important role. Modern education has encouraged a completely lopsided development of this aspect of the mind. The essence of the intellect is to divide. So humanity has embarked on a journey of wholesale division, discrimination, and dissection. We have split everything. Even the invisible atom has been split.

Once you unleash the intellect, it splits everything it encounters; it does not allow you to *be* with anything totally.

Although it is a wonderful instrument for survival, it is also at the same time a terrible barrier that stands between you and your experience of the oneness of life.

How do we address this problem?

Yoga offers us a way. In our times, it is not just a useful strategy; it is perhaps our *only* chance of reversing a journey that seems to be taking us headlong toward self-destruction.

The intellect is becoming a barrier because you keep it constantly dipped in the accumulative part of the mind—your memory, manas. Examine this for yourself. You will find that *every* thought that arises in the mind has its roots in data you have already accumulated. The data may be gathered consciously or unconsciously. In any case, this basically means your intellect is perpetually immersed in the past. In such a state, nothing new is now possible. And so, the intellect loses its edge and becomes a trap.

The accumulative part of the mind is, to put it simply, just society's garbage bin. It is merely a heap of impressions you have gathered from outside. Anybody you encounter stuffs something into your head and moves on: your parents, teachers, friends, enemies, preachers, the news anchor on TV, just about everyone. You have no choice about who to receive from and who not to receive from. The moment you say "I don't like this person," you often end up receiving much more from him or her than anybody else! You have the ability to process the information you receive, but that is all. Your ability to merely recycle the garbage you have picked up is what the mighty intellect has been reduced to.

The blitzkrieg of information that your mind receives daily enters you only through your five sense organs. Your sense organs, as we have seen before, always perceive everything only in comparison. Where there is comparison, there is always duality. Suppose I were to show you my hand. While you are able to see one side, you cannot see the other. If I were to show you the other side, you would not be able to perceive this first side. Human perception through the sense organs is always piecemeal. It can give you an illusion of completeness but can never comprehend the whole.

When you keep your intellect dipped in this limited, fragmented, accumulative dimension of your mind, you draw conclusions about life that are completely distorted. The more people become engrossed in thought, the more joyless they become. It is unfortunate. But let me be clear: thought in itself is not a problem. People who think with clarity should be joyful. Unfortunately, for many people, the more they think, the more incapable they become of smiling! The problem is just that they have enslaved their faculty of discernment to the limitations of their sense perception.

But the same intellect can be sharpened if you allow it to soak in the other aspect of your mind—your awareness, chitta. If you want to reach your ultimate nature through the mind, you need to make the intellect *truly* discriminatory, in the ultimate sense. This does not mean dividing everything into good and bad, right and wrong, high and low, heaven and hell, sacred and profane. Instead, all it means is learning to *discern the real from the illusory, what is existentially true from what is psychologically true.*

If you soak your intellect in your awareness, the discerning dimension of your mind can turn into a miraculous tool of liberation. It can become razor-sharp, slice through what is true and untrue, and deliver you to a different dimension of life altogether.

Learn to place your intellect in the sheath of your awareness rather than in the sack of memory and identification. Once you do, this tremendous instrument can cut its way effortlessly toward the ultimate.

Sadhana

If you consciously walk a tightrope, you have no choice but to be aware. If your intellect is constantly choosing between good and bad, it has become a prejudiced intellect. And when it is busy sorting the world into good and bad, you will most definitely fall off the tightrope. Don't take the tightrope literally. You could just try bringing a certain precision into the physical movements of the body. (If you have a hatha yoga practice, it should happen anyway.) For instance, if you see a straight line on the floor, try walking in perfect alignment with that line, maintaining an easy gait. This is not about becoming self-conscious, but about becoming precise or exact. Try this with your body and see. Bring precision into every movement, every gesture. This is one way of dipping your intellect in awareness.

Awareness Is Aliveness

What do we mean by the word "awareness," anyway? What does it signify? And how can we access it?

First and foremost, let us make an important distinction: awareness is not mental alertness. Mental alertness will only enhance your ability to survive in the world. It is a doglike alertness—useful in self-preservation but not in self-expansion. Awareness is not something that you *do*. Awareness is what you are. Awareness is aliveness.

The dimension of the mind that modern societies have completely ignored at their own peril is awareness, or chitta. This is intelligence that is completely unsullied by memory. This is the deepest dimension of the mind and one that connects you with that which is the very basis of creation. When you are in touch with this dimension, you are in a state of heightened awareness, which allows you to be fully conscious and intoxicated at the same time—and with no external stimulus whatsoever! When you learn to access chitta, being blissful is entirely natural.

Sleep, wakefulness, death—these are all just different levels of awareness. Suppose you were dozing and somebody shook you awake. *Boom!* The whole world comes back in a single moment! That is not a small thing. You re-created the whole of existence instantly. The world, which was obliterated in your experience, pops back. Not in seven days—*in just a moment*.

How do you know whether the world exists or not? Only by your experience. There is no other proof. So, awareness is that which can either create or obliterate this existence. That is the magic of awareness.

You can pitch your awareness up to different levels. As you notch it up further and further, whole new dimensions of existence open up in your experience. Worlds that nobody had imagined in their wildest possible dreams become a living reality for you.

When you are asleep, the world does not exist because you are largely unaware. But even in sleep, you are not completely unaware. The difference between a sleeping person and a dead person is one of awareness. Similarly, between a wakeful person and an awakened or enlightened person, there is a difference. An awakened person sleeps too, but has managed so much awareness that some part of him or her does not sleep. The sense organs shut down, the body rests a bit, but everything else is on. This is because awareness has been notched up to another level.

Awareness is a process of inclusiveness, a way of embracing this entire existence. You cannot *do* it, but you can set the right conditions so that it happens. Don't try to *be* aware. It will not work. If you keep your body, thought, emotion, and energies properly aligned, awareness will blossom. You will become far more alive than you are right now.

When you are consciously in touch with your awareness, you gain access to the subtlest dimension of physicality, or *akash*. As we have seen before, the universe is just a play of five elements—water, fire, earth, air, and ether. Creation is just a frolic of these five. It is ether that we refer to as "akash" in yogic terminology, and each human being has a certain dimension of this fifth element around him or her. While the other elements are within the body, the akashic, or etheric, dimension envelops the physical body—usually up to a distance of eighteen to twenty-one inches. Because this element is still physical, it carries information. Anything that happens at a certain level of intensity or profundity in your life is written into this field of akash around you.

When you gain conscious access to your awareness, you gain access to the akashic dimension around your body, as also to the akashic dimension around the planet, the solar system, and the entire universe. Without any of the instruments of modern technology, the ancients in India and some other parts of the world amassed a remarkable amount of knowledge about the cosmos. All this was gleaned through the dimension of *chidakash,* or the akashic dimension of our intelligence.

Once you are in touch with your awareness, you don't have to *try* to accomplish anything. You don't even have to wish or dream, because the best possible thing that can happen to you *will* happen. In the yogic lore, it is said that when you learn to access this dimension, you have enslaved the divine! God works for you from now on. What exactly does this mean? This means that once you distance yourself from the compulsiveness of your own genetic and karmic information, life becomes unburdened, flexible, incredibly effortless. This is a dimension beyond intellect, beyond identification, beyond memory, beyond judgment, beyond karma, beyond divisions of every kind. This is the intelligence of existence itself, in which life always happens exactly the way it should, with absolute and unfaltering ease.

Sadhana

—⟨∞⟩—

If you are aware at the moment of death, you will be aware beyond death also. Start practicing with sleep. Sleep is nothing but temporary death. Every night you are presented with a tremendous possibility—the possibility of becoming aware of the dimension beyond death.

You can try this experiment tonight. At the moment that you move from wakefulness to sleep, make an attempt to be aware. This practice can be done in bed. If you can be aware of the last moment when you make the transition from wakefulness to sleep, you will be aware throughout your sleep.

You will see it is a lot of work. So here is another thing you can do. If you are used to waking up to an alarm, substitute it with a sound, a tune, or chant that reminds you of your awareness. You can easily train yourself to make this association. It can become an alarm for your awareness.

Of course, you cannot use an alarm to go to sleep! But the fact of the matter is that unless you completely dis-identify from your body, it is not easy to move consciously from wakefulness to sleep. The first possible moment that you come awake, see if you can become consciously aware of something—your breath or your body, for instance. This will help you later when you want to go to bed.

If you achieve waking with awareness and moving from wakefulness to sleep in awareness, you are deathless. This means that when it comes to shedding the body, you will do it in full awareness. Even getting close to that moment will change the

way your body and mind function, and will alter the quality of
your life quite phenomenally.

Knowing Without Thought

Have you ever watched a beehive closely? It doesn't matter
whether you have studied the most advanced level of engineering, there is still something to learn from a beehive. What a
fabulous feat of engineering it is! This is truly the best apart-
ment complex you could imagine, exquisitely designed and
structured, and amazingly resilient. In no kind of weather
have you ever seen a beehive falling off a tree, have you?

Although it is a magnificent piece of work, do the bees
have engineering plans in their heads? No. These plans are
there in their *bodies*. They know exactly what to do because
of a blueprint in their systems.

Spiritual knowledge or "knowing" was always transmitted
like this—not by thought, not by word, but in the same way
that bees transmit the understanding of how to build beehives
across generations. Once this knowing is transmitted or
"downloaded," as it were, everything that you need to know is
right within you. When you download a certain type of software onto your computer, you don't have to understand how
all of it works. You don't have to read every word that is written in the software. You press one key, and it produces a result;
another key, another result. Suddenly, you have a different
kind of phenomenon.

I make a distinction between knowledge and knowing.
Knowledge is essentially accumulated information. All infor-

mation is only related to the physical nature of existence. Knowing, on the other hand, is a living intelligence. With or without you, it still *is*. You are either in it or you are not: that is the only choice you have.

There is an intrinsic intelligence within you that, as we have seen earlier, is capable of transforming a piece of bread into a human being. The most sophisticated machine, including the brain, was created by this intrinsic intelligence. Right now you are just trying to use a limited section of your brain, and you think that is intelligence. No. There is something within you that can create an entire human brain in all its magnificent complexity and capability. That "something" functions in an altogether different way. For example, I don't think with my head but with *every cell in my body*. This makes my thinking an organic, seamless, and integrated process. There is a certain level of integratedness about it, because it involves all of me. I don't have much thought in my mind at all, unless I choose to think.

Nothing has ever been out of place in this existence. Things have only been out of place in human societies. Between this piece of life and that piece of life, there can be a comparison. But for the intelligence that is making all life happen, there is no context, no comparison, because there is no other. You cannot say whether it is now in place or not—it is *always* in place. There is no other way for it to be.

And the pursuit of yoga is just this: moving from this small headful of information to a cosmos of intelligence. What a tragic choice people so often end up making—choosing the finiteness of the human brain over a universe of infinite knowing.

Sadhana

⸺⸙⸺

Just work at removing from the mind the idea that thought is intelligence. The whole process of creation, from a single atom to the cosmos, is a fantastic expression of intelligence. Right now within your own body, there is a throbbing intelligence that is the very source of creation. With the overrated intellect that you own, can you even understand the activity of a single cell in your body in its entirety? The first step toward moving from the trap of the intellect to the lap of a larger intelligence is to recognize that every aspect of life—from a grain of sand to a mountain, a drop to an ocean, from the atomic to the cosmic—is a manifestation of a far greater intelligence than your minuscule intellect. If you take this one step, life will start speaking to you like never before.

Believing versus Seeking

Once it happened . . . On a certain day, two Irishmen were working on the street, in front of a London brothel. They saw a Protestant minister coming their way. He rolled up his collar, put his head down, and quietly slipped into the brothel.

The two men looked at each other and shrugged. "See, what else can you expect from a Protestant?"

They continued to work. After some time a rabbi came by. He had a muffler around his throat, almost covering his face. He ducked into the brothel too. The men were deeply pained and shook their heads sadly. "What has happened? Times have gone bad. A religious man in a brothel! Why is this happening?"

After a while the local bishop came along. He looked this way and that, tightened his cloak around himself, and slipped into the brothel.

One of the men turned to the other and said, "One of the girls must be really sick."

The moment you get strongly identified, you lose your perspective on life! Ideas of good and bad, right and wrong are all your mental constructs. They have nothing to do with life as such. What was considered to be moral a hundred years ago is intolerable today. What you think is very good, your children despise. Your ideas of good and bad are just a certain level of prejudice against life.

The moment you get identified with your limited ideas of morality you become completely twisted. Your intellect functions around these identifications in such a way that you never see the world as it is. If you want an element of spirituality to enter your life, the first thing you must do is drop these rigid ideas of virtue and vice, and learn to look at life just the way it is.

One of the biggest problems in the world today is that right from a person's childhood, an inflexible system of morality has been imposed on the mind. Whatever you consider good, you naturally get identified with it. Whatever you consider bad, you are naturally repelled by. This attraction and aversion is the basis of all strong identification. The nature of your mind is that whatever you are averse to dominates it. Moralists and preachers have for generations told humanity to eschew "evil thoughts." That is a surefire strategy to achieve the reverse! Now, if you try to resist that supposedly "evil thought," it becomes a full-time job. There is nothing else going on in your head.

The idea of moral superiority has been the source of too many inhuman acts to be ignored. Most people who believe they are virtuous are hard to live with. Besides, they spend most of their lives trying to avoid what they consider "wrong" or "sinful." That usually means they are constantly thinking about it. Avoiding something is not freedom from it. Such morality is based on exclusion. Spirituality, on the other hand, is born of inclusion.

The essential nature of our humanity has been so suppressed and distorted that the substitute of "morality" has been brought in to bring some order and sanity to our lives. This has happened because we have not done anything to keep our humanity active. If your humanity were active, there would be no need for morality at all.

Morality always differs from person to person, according to time, place, situation—and convenience. But wherever humanity has found its expression, at any time in history or in any culture in the world, it has always been the same and will always be. On a superficial level, in terms of our values, morals, and ethics, each one of us may be different. But if you know how to pierce a person deep enough to touch this humanity, each one of us is the same.

To impose morality, you don't need any involvement with people; you just have to dole out the diktats: "Be good; speak kindly; if you speak in anger, the consequences will be dire," and so forth. But if you want to kindle the humanity in a person, it takes much more involvement. It means giving *yourself*.

Morality is worthwhile because it helps ensure social order, but it is capable of wreaking inner havoc. Since nobody can live by the morals prescribed by most religions, most of humanity lives in a state of perpetual guilt, shame, and fear. This is a tragically crippled existence. Humanity will also bring social order, but it requires no external enforcement whatsoever.

Make a list of all the things that the major religions of the world call a "sin," and you will find that just to be alive is a sin. If you are born it is a sin; if you menstruate, it is a sin; if you copulate, it is a sin. Forget all this, even if you so much as eat a chocolate, you could commit a sin. Since the very process of life is a sin, you live in perennial guilt and terror. If people were not so wracked by fear and guilt, the temples, mosques, and churches in the world would not be as congested as they are now. If you were naturally joyful, you would go and sit on the beach, or listen to the whisper of the leaves on the tree. Only because religions have instilled such a sense of fear and shame are you ashamed of your very biology! Now you have to go to someplace that is considered "holy" to wash it off.

People will always find ways to subvert values, morals, and ethics. But when you are naturally joyful, you are naturally pleasant with the world around you. Spirituality does not mean moving away from life; it means becoming alive to the core, in the fullest possible way. With age, physical agility may diminish, but the level of joy and aliveness need not. If your level of joy and aliveness is declining, you are committing suicide in installments.

Unfortunately, all kinds of belief systems are passed off as spirituality today. The spiritual process is always a quest. There is a significant difference between *believing* and *seeking*. Believing means you have assumed something that you do not know; seeking means you have realized that you do not know. This brings an enormous amount of flexibility. The moment you believe something, you bring a certain rigidity into the very life process that you are. This rigidity is not just in attitude; it percolates into every aspect of your life and is the cause of an enormous amount of suffering in the world. Human society reflects the inner experience of human beings. Creating human beings who are flexible and willing to look at everything in a fresh, unprejudiced way, rather than being stuck in beliefs and opinions, definitely makes for a different kind of society.

Yoga is a method that has worked wonderfully for me, and for millions of people. It is an entirely scientific method that originates not in faith or belief but in a profound understanding of the human mechanism. Nor does it come from some naïve sense of optimism. The premise is simple: if you have a good seed and if you create the right atmosphere, it will sprout. Creating the right atmosphere of body and mind is the only work. You do not have to do anything else. No teachings of morality, no metaphysical discourses are needed. If your humanity is stirred, you are a beautiful human being.

All that is considered to be negative in the world actually springs from limitation. A limited identity that we impose upon ourselves is what sets us up as "me" versus the "other." It is in this space of division and separation that all crime and negativity is born. So, striving for the infinite is an insurance against all negative tendencies. As a race, humanity now needs to liberate life, rather than control it. From limitation to liberation—this is the way.

The Wishing Tree

Your mind can be in five different states. It could be inert—meaning, it is not activated at all; it is in a rudimentary state. If you energize it, it becomes active but scattered. If you energize it further, it is no longer scattered, but starts oscillating. If you energize it further, it becomes one-pointed. If you energize it still further, it will become conscious. And if your mind is conscious, it is magic; it is a miracle; it is a bridge to the beyond.

Inert minds are not a problem. Someone who is very simpleminded and whose intellect is still not effervescent has no trouble. He eats well and sleeps well. It is only people who think too much who cannot eat and sleep properly! Simpleminded people perform all the activities of the body far better than the so-called intellectuals of the world. There is a certain peace in them because you need some intelligence to create disturbance and chaos. An inert mind is closer to animal nature than the human.

The moment you pump in some energy, the mind becomes active, but it is often scattered. When some people begin their spiritual practices, they may experience a new level of effervescence that they may not be able to handle, unless they are in congenial atmospheres. They may interpret this mental effervescence, powered by new energy levels in the system, as disturbance. There is a pervasive paranoia among people, a tendency to fear everything that is new. But in reality, all they are doing is moving from inertness toward a higher level of aliveness.

Once those who have very scattered minds start spiritual practices, they reach a place where the mind becomes less diffuse. But now it starts oscillating—one day, it moves this way; another day, the other way. This is, however, a huge improvement over being scattered, where the mind moves every moment across ten different places.

If the mind was already oscillating and is energized further, then slowly it becomes concentrated, or, as we say in yoga, "one-pointed." That is far better than the previous state. But the highest state is when the mind becomes *conscious*. In terms of instruments, it is not your computer, car, or spacecraft, but the human mind that is the most miraculous—if only you could use it consciously. The reason why success comes so easily and naturally for one person, and is a struggle for someone else, is essentially this: one person has organized his or her mind to think the way he wants, and another thinks against his or her own interests.

A well-established human mind is referred to as a *kalpavriksha,* or a wishing tree that grants any boon. With such a mind, whatever you ask for becomes a reality. All you need to do is to develop the mind to a point where it becomes a wishing tree, rather than a source of madness. A mind that can manifest whatever it chooses is described in yoga as being in a state of *samyukti*. This is a skillfulness that arises out of equanimity.

Once your thoughts get organized, your emotions will also

get organized. Gradually, your energies and body get organized in the same direction as well. However, the order in which you address these dimensions could vary, depending on what you are ready for. Considering the realities of the day, most people are not ready for any system unless they are first intellectually convinced of it. Eventually, once your thoughts, emotions, body, and energy are channeled in one direction, your ability to create and manifest what you want is incredible.

Today modern science is proving that this whole existence is just a reverberation of energy, an endless vibration. Thoughts too are a reverberation. If you generate a powerful thought and let it out, it will always manifest itself. For this to happen, it is important that you do not impede and weaken your thought by creating negative and self-defeating thought patterns.

Generally, people use faith as a means to banish negative thoughts. Once you become a thinking human being, however, doubts invariably surface. The way your mind is made, if God appears right here this moment, you will not surrender to him or her. Instead, you will want to conduct an investigation to find out whether this is the genuine article or not.

There is an alternative to faith, which is *commitment*. If you simply commit yourself to creating what you really care for, now once again your thoughts get organized in such a way that there are no hurdles. Your thoughts flow freely toward what you want, and once this happens, the manifestation of your desire is a natural consequence.

To create what you really care for, your desire must first be well manifested in your mind. Is that what you *really* want? Think this through carefully. How many times in your life have you thought, "This is it." The moment you got there you realized that was not it at all! So, first explore what it is that you really want. Once that is clear and you are committed to creating it, you generate a continuous process of thought in that direction. When you maintain a steady stream of thought without changing direction, it will manifest as a reality in your life.

There are yogic processes by which you can touch another dimension of intelligence, unsullied by memory, called chitta, which we have mentioned earlier. Realizing the power of chitta is called *chit shakti,* a simple and powerful process through which you can access the very source of creation within you.

The Myth of Head versus Heart

It is common to hear people say that their head leads them in one direction and their heart in another. In yoga, the fundamental basis we establish is this: you are one person, a single, unified being. There is no separation of head and heart; you are one whole.

Let us first understand what is being referred to as the "head" and the "heart." You usually assign your thoughts to the head and your emotions to the heart. But if you look at this carefully and with absolute sincerity, you will realize that the way you think is the way you feel. But it is also true that the way you feel is the way you think. This is why yoga includes both thought and emotion as part of the same *manomayakosha,* or mental body.

What you normally think of as "mind" is the thought process or intellect. But in fact, the mind has many dimensions: one is the logical aspect; another is the deeper emotional aspect. The intellect, as we know, is termed buddhi. The deeper dimension of the mind is conventionally known as the heart. But in yoga this deeper emotional mind is known as manas. Manas is a complex amalgam of memory that molds emotions in a particular way. So, the way you feel and the way you think are both activities of the mind.

It is quite simple. If I think you are a wonderful person, I will have sweet emotions toward you. If I think you are a horrible person, I will harbor nasty emotions about you. If you make someone your enemy and then try to love him or her, that is hard work. Let us not make hard work of the simple aspects of life.

The way you think is the way you feel, but thought and feeling seem to be different in your experience. Why is this so? Because thought has a certain clarity, a certain agility about it. Emotion is slower. Today, you think this is a very wonderful person and you have warm feelings about him. Suddenly, he does something that you don't like, and you think he is horrible. Your thought tells you he is horrible, but your emotion cannot change immediately. It struggles. If it is sweet now, it cannot turn bitter at the very next moment. It takes time to turn around. It has a wider turning arc. Depending on the strength of your emotion, maybe it will take three days or three months or three years, but after some time, it will turn around.

It is not useful to create this conflict between head and heart. Emotion is just the juicier part of thought. You can enjoy its sweetness, but it is largely the thought that leads the emotion, whether you recognize it or not. Emotion is not entirely steady. Your emotion also chatters, goes this way and that, but it is less agile than thought. Since it takes longer to turn, and its intensity is usually substantially greater than thought, it often seems as though thought and emotion are different. But they are no more separate than sugarcane and its juice.

Thought is not as intense as emotion in most people's experience. (You usually do not think as intensely as you get angry, for instance.) But if you generate an intense enough thought, it can also overwhelm you. Only five to ten percent of the population may be capable of generating the kind of thought that is so intense that there is no need for emotion. Ninety percent of the population can only generate intense emotions because they have never done the necessary work in the other direction. But there are people whose thought is very deep. They don't have much emotion, but they are very deep thinkers.

It is best not to create polarities within yourself. That makes for civil war and schizophrenia. Thought and feeling are not different. One is dry. Another is juicy. Enjoy both.

Knowing and Devotion

In the yogic culture, there are two aspects to the word *shi-va*. The word literally means "that which is not." Everything that *is* has come from "that which is not." If you look up at the sky, you will see many stars and celestial objects, but still the biggest presence out there is a vast emptiness. It is in the lap of this no-thingness that the dance of creation is happening right now. This emptiness, which is the very basis of creation, is referred to as "shi-va."

Another dimension of Shiva is Adiyogi, the first yogi, who opened up the incredible science of yoga for humanity. The yogic culture moves seamlessly from invoking shi-va as the basis of creation to invoking Shiva as the first yogi. Thus shi-va becomes personified as Shiva.

Is this contradictory?

Not at all. Because once yoga or ultimate union has happened, there is no longer a distinction between ultimate reality and the one who has experienced it. In accordance with this logic, the yogic culture offers two ways to reach the ultimate state: becoming everything or becoming nothing; the path of *gnana,* knowing, or the path of *bhakti,* devotion.

If you want to experience shi-va, or the dimension beyond the physical, you either come to terms with the laws that govern the non-physical realm or you dissolve into this dimension, because it spells freedom from the laws that govern the physical realm. If you want to experience a mountain peak, you either elevate yourself to that level, or simply look up. These are the two fundamental ways. Otherwise, no meeting is possible. Through knowledge, you aspire to meet "that which is not" face-to-face. Through devotion, you strive to obliterate your limited and rigid persona and move toward a more flexible state from which you approach the dimension beyond the framework of your likes and dislikes. These likes and dislikes are the very basis of your persona. The endless nature of human desire is an expression of longing for infinite nature or life beyond physical existence. Infinity and zero are just positive and negative expressions of the same reality.

Devotion means dropping the dualities of like and dislike, attachment and aversion. It means "what's fine" and "what's not fine" do not exist for you anymore; *everything* is fine. When a devotee says "God is everywhere" or "everything is God," he is essentially saying "everything is fine." Thus, he or she arrives at a deep state of acceptance that is transformative and liberating. Bhakti is all-encompassing and all-inclusive; it does not discriminate. This is the nature of the ultimate reality as well.

Since ancient times, devotion has been seen as the most important spiritual path, because it is the quickest. But it has its own pitfalls. The path of knowing is harder, but it is an "eyes-open" path. Devotion, on the other hand, is an "eyes-closed" path. With knowing, every step you take, forward or backward, you know where you are going. With devotion, whether you are moving toward your liberation or you have fallen into a pit, you have no clue.

Generally, for most people, emotion is more intense than thought. That is why devotion has been glorified above all other paths. But without the right understanding and wisdom, walking the path of devotion can lead to all kinds of delusions. Devotion is a tool to transcend the dual nature of logic. But instead of transcending logic, one may end up denying logic altogether. So, standing on a stable platform of logic before going into the fluid state of devotion becomes important.

Conversely, many people believe that devotion has no place

in the logical realm. But this is not true. Logic is essentially a cutting tool, an instrument of discernment. If your logic is like a machete, when you consider something, it will fall into two pieces. But if the scalpel of logic you employ is very finely honed, you can cut through something, and still seem to leave it in one piece. When a fine swordsman uses his sword to cut a tree, it is said even the tree should not know; it should still stand as one. If your intellect becomes this refined, you will find devotion fits in perfectly with your logic.

Devotion can be very beautiful, joyous, ecstatic, but without the clarity of knowing, it could lead to stagnation. On the other hand, without emotion, spiritual practices can become barren, dry, and lifeless. Without bhakti, gnana becomes simply a hairsplitting exercise.

As I said earlier, if you want to experience a mountain peak, you either elevate yourself to that level, or simply look up. The devotee knows that if you manage to ascend to meet the peak, you still only stand *beside* the peak. But if you become the valley, you hold the entire mountain in your lap.

YOGA AND INTOXICATION

According to legend, Adiyogi drank *somarasa*, the intoxicating juice of the moon. He simply imbibed the distilled essence of the moonbeams and was described as constantly drunk.

Yogis are not against pleasure. They are unwilling to settle for little pleasures, that's all! They know if you drink a glass of wine, it just gives you a buzz, but to-morrow morning it gives you a headache and more. Yogis are not willing to settle for that. To enjoy intoxi-cation you must be totally drunk yet fully alert. I have never touched any substance, but if you look into my eyes you will see that I am always stoned. I am totally drunk and fully aware. This is one of the pleasures that the science of yoga offers.

The end goal is not just intoxication. This blissful state eliminates the fear of suffering. In this state of nameless ecstasy, there are no concerns about self-preservation. This is what makes a human being capa-ble of being and acting in a way that can sometimes seem superhuman to others.

Only when the gnawing anxiety of self-preservation is completely eliminated from your mind would you dare to explore life. Otherwise you only want to protect it. Once the fear of suffering is dropped, you can plunge into any situation without hesitation. Even if you are damned to eternal hell, you will happily go there be-cause you have no fear of suffering!

When everybody was talking about going to heaven, Gautama the Buddha said, "You say everything is fine in heaven, so what will I do there? Let me go to hell and do something to help others, because anyway I cannot suffer."

As long as the fear of suffering persists, you will not dare to explore the deeper dimensions of life. Only this body needs to be protected; nothing else within you needs protection. If you are willing to drop the ideas, philosophies, and belief systems you are currently attached to, you can re-create your entire life with the very next moment.

Love Mantra

And what about love? Is there such a thing as unconditional love? Can it truly exist between two human beings? These are frequently asked questions.

One day Shankaran Pillai went to a park. He saw an attractive woman seated on a stone bench. He settled down on the same bench. After a few minutes he moved a little closer. She moved away. He waited for a few minutes, then moved a little closer; she moved away. When he did this again, she moved to the very end of the bench. He went very close and put his arm around her. She shoved him away. Then he went down on his knees, plucked a flower, handed it to her, and said, "I love you like I have never loved anybody in my life."

The sun was setting. He had a flower in his hand. He looked at her with a melting gaze. Above all, the ambience was right. She thawed. Nature took over and they had their way with each other. The dusk deepened into night. Shankaran Pillai suddenly sprang to his feet and said, "It's eight o'clock. I need to go."

She said, "What? Now? You just said you loved me more than anyone else!"

"Yes, yes, of course, but my wife will be waiting."

Generally, we have made relationships within frameworks

that are comfortable and profitable for us. People have physical, psychological, emotional, financial, and social needs to fulfill. To fulfill these needs, one of the best ways is to tell someone, "I love you." This so-called love has become something of an "open sesame" mantra. You can get what you want by saying it.

Love is a quality, not something to do with somebody else. Every action that we do is in some way to fulfill certain needs. If you see this, then there is a possibility that you can grow into love as your natural quality. But you can go on fooling yourself into believing that the relationships you have made for convenience, comfort, and well-being are actually relationships of love. I am not saying there is no experience of love at all in these associations, but it is within certain limitations. It does not matter how many times true love has been proclaimed; if a few expectations and requirements are not fulfilled, things fall apart. This is essentially a mutual benefit scheme.

There is really no such thing as conditional love and unconditional love. There are conditions and there is love. When you talk about love, it *has* to be unconditional. The moment there is a condition, it just amounts to a transaction. Maybe a convenient transaction, maybe a good arrangement, but that will not fulfill you or transport you to another dimension. It is just convenient. Love need not necessarily be convenient; most of the time it is not. It takes *life*. You have to invest *yourself*.

If you have to be in love, you should not *be*. The English expression "falling in love" is very significant. You don't climb in love, you don't stand in love, you don't fly in love, you *fall* in love. Something of you should fall or melt away to accommodate the other. There is a distinction between a transaction and a love affair. A love affair need not be with any particular person; you could be having a great love affair with life itself.

What you do or do not do is in accordance with the circumstances you are in. Our actions are always molded by the demands of external situations. But love is an inner state, and how you are within yourself can definitely be unconditional. Acts of love can become tedious and stressful over a period of time. You realize love is not something that you do; love is the way you are.

Sadhana

Love is never between two people. It is what happens within you, and your interiority need not be enslaved to someone or something else. Try this for fifteen minutes or so: go sit with something that means nothing to you right now—maybe a tree, a pebble, a worm, or an insect. Do it a few days in a row. After a while, you will find you can look upon it with as much love as you do your wife or husband or mother or child. Maybe the worm does not know this. That doesn't matter. If you can look at everything lovingly, the whole world becomes beautiful in your experience.

Devotion: A Dimensional Shift

Most people live cautiously, measuring out their love and joy in sparing doses for fear that it will run out. The most generous way to live is to set an example to the rest of the world by living life full-throttle and beyond all limitations. If you are so stingy that you cannot love, laugh, or live totally, you are a *kanjoos*—a miser—on all levels! Devotion means you are not a kanjoos—you are full of juice! A devotee is someone who seeks to explore and experience life as fully as possible.

Devotion is not a dissection of life, but a total embrace. It is not a love affair, but a crazy business. Love itself is crazy, but there are shreds of sanity attached to it; you can still recover. In devotion, there is no shred of sanity; there is no way to recover. Devotees have the sweetest experience of life. Everybody may think they are idiots, but they are having the best time on the planet. You decide who the idiot is!

When I say "devotion," I am not talking about faith or belief. Belief is just like morality. People who believe something often think they are superior to others. All that happens the moment you believe something is that your stupidity acquires confidence. Confidence and stupidity are a very dangerous combination, but they generally go together. If you start looking at the world around you, you would clearly understand that what you know is so minuscule that there is no way to act with confidence. A belief system takes away this problem; it gives you enormous confidence, but it does not cure your stupidity.

Devotion is not an act; it is not directed toward one thing or another; the *object* of devotion is immaterial. It is just that with devotion you have dissolved all the resistance in you so that the divine can transpire as effortlessly as breath. The divine is not an entity sitting up there; it is a living force every moment of your life. Devotion makes you aware of this.

Once it happened . . . At a traditional Catholic family dinner, the man of the house came to the table, looked at the food, and, as usual, grumbled and cursed his wife and everything around him. After the cursing was over and everyone settled down, he sat down and uttered his prayer, "Dear God, thank you for the daily bread and all the wonderful things on the table."

His five-year-old girl sat meekly at the table. You know, these five-year-olds—extra pillows and little cushions are always kept for them, but still they can never really reach the plate. So, this little five-year-old girl, with the table up to her neck, squeaked, "Daddy, does God hear all our prayers?"

Immediately, the Christian in him awakened and he said, "Yes, of course. Every prayer we utter, He always hears."

Then the girl sank a little lower, because she sank into her thoughts. After a while, she said, "But, Daddy, does He also listen to all the other things that we say?"

"Yes, every moment of our lives God is listening to everything that we say and do."

Then she sank a little lower and said, "Daddy, then which does He believe?"

Tell me, which should God believe—your prayers or your curses? He must be thoroughly confused! He must have given up. Because we systematize or institutionalize the most subtle parts of life, suddenly everything loses its vibrancy and becomes lifeless. The same words are being uttered, parrot-like, by everybody, but they do not mean anything anymore. When we say something that does not really mean anything to us, that does not burn within us, it is tantamount to a lie. It is actually better to shut up.

We are always trying to mimic those whom we consider to be our mentors and role models. When somebody said something similar two thousand years ago it worked for him—because of the fire in his heart, because of the truth that was burning within him, not because of the words he uttered.

There is nothing tame or tepid about devotion. It is not for the lily-livered. It is hot. Devotion scorches.

AKKA MAHADEVI

Around nine hundred years ago in southern India, there lived a female mystic called Akka Mahadevi. Akka was a devotee of Shiva. Ever since her childhood, she had regarded Shiva as her beloved, her husband. It was not just a belief; for her it was a living reality.

The king saw this beautiful young woman one day, and decided he wanted her as his wife. She refused. But the king was adamant and threatened her parents, so she yielded.

She married the man, but she kept him at a physical distance. He tried to woo her, but her constant refrain was, "Shiva is my husband." Time passed and the king's patience wore thin. Infuriated, he tried to lay his hands upon her. She refused. "I have another husband. His name is Shiva. He visits me, and I am with him. I cannot be with you."

Because she claimed to have another husband, she was brought to court for prosecution. Akka is said to have announced to all present, "Being a queen doesn't mean a thing to me. I will leave."

When the king saw the ease with which she was walking away from everything, he made a last futile effort to salvage his dignity. He said, "Everything on your person—your jewels, your garments—belongs to me. Leave it all here and go."

So, in the full assembly, Akka just dropped her jewelry, all her clothes, and walked away naked. From that day on, she refused to wear clothes even though many tried to convince her otherwise. It was unbelievable for a woman to be walking naked on the streets of India at the time—and this was a beautiful young woman. She lived out her life as a wandering mendicant and composed some exquisite poetry that lives on to this very day.

In a poem (translated by A. K. Ramanujan), she says:

People,
male and female,
blush when a cloth covering their shame
comes loose.
When the lord of lives
lives drowned without a face
in the world, how can you be modest?

When all the world is the eye of the lord,
onlooking everywhere, what can you
cover and conceal?

Devotees of this kind may be in this world but not of it. The power and passion with which they lived their lives make them inspirations for generations of humanity. Akka continues to be a living presence in the Indian collective consciousness, and her lyrical poems remain among the most prized works of South Indian literature to this very day.

Embracing Mystery

It is only a juvenile intelligence that analyzes things and arrives at a conclusion. If your intelligence is sufficiently evolved and mature, you realize that the more you analyze, the further away you are from any conclusion.

If you go deeply into any aspect of life, you will move further and further away from any conclusion. Life becomes more mysterious than ever before. The more you delve into life, you see that it is an endless and unfathomable process. You cannot get it because you are it. When you realize experientially that every atom, every grain of sand, every pebble, every piece of life from the smallest to the biggest is unfathomable, you will naturally bow down in utmost devotion to everything. If you simply sit here and breathe, you will know life better than through any deep analysis.

As we dissect everything, wanting to excavate truth from physical nature, we enter into the minute dimensions of particle science. From protons, neutrons, and electrons to neutrinos, bosons, and super-symmetric particles, we seem to be going deeper and deeper. But all this is still only in the realm of physical nature. Dark matter, we are told, comprises more of the universe than matter—and this dark matter is not composed of atoms at all but of particles of a still unknown type.

Pick up a glass of water and take a look at it. What do you really know about it? Why, for instance, do hydrogen and oxygen combine to become water? Or pick up a pebble and gaze at it long and hard. Why does it have this particular shape, size, grain, texture? Or just look at yourself: why are you the way you are? Many would reply, "Oh, my father, my mother—and here I am." But why are you like this? What is the basis of this form, this body, this individuality?

Traditionally in India, it was said that one ought to bow down to everything that one encountered. It did not matter if it was a tree or a cow or a snake or a cloud—you just bowed down to it. When you bow to everything, it could be because you are a fool, or because you have looked at life in its utmost profundity. The difference between an idiot and an enlightened being is thin. The two often look similar, but they are actually worlds apart. An idiot is incapable of drawing conclusions. A mystic is unwilling to draw conclusions. The rest have glorified their conclusions as knowledge. The fool just enjoys whatever little he knows and one who has seen life in its utmost depth enjoys it absolutely. The rest are the ones who constantly struggle and suffer.

One morning a man walked into his office and told his boss, "Boss, I want you to know, three big companies are after me. You must give me a raise."

His boss said, "What! Which companies? Who wants you?"

He said, "The electric company, the telephone company, and the gas company."

Something is always behind the so-called smart people, those with confirmed conclusions about life! Or else, they are always busy chasing something. An idiot can sit here quietly. A mystic can sit here quietly. The rest cannot.

Devotion is a simple method of dissolving all the hurdles on the path. If those who are struggling to contain the chattering of the "monkey mind" become devoted, the chatter will just evaporate.

If you learn to bow, to hold everything higher than yourself, it does not seem to be good for your self-esteem. But becoming a devotee does not mean you are a pushover. That which knows how to bend will not break. (That is why you are encouraged to do your hatha yoga every morning—essentially so your body does not break!) That is so with everything within you.

Unfortunately, these days even so-called spiritual leaders are talking about self-esteem. "Self" and "esteem" are both a problem. Both are very limited entities; both are fragile; both will always be insecure. If you have no esteem, very good. If you have no self, fabulous!

Sadhana

When you experience something as far bigger than yourself, bowing down will naturally occur to you. If you want to become a devotee, at least once an hour in all the waking moments of your life, put your hands together and bow to something. It does not matter who or what. Don't choose. Whatever you see, just bow your head—whether it is a tree, a mountain, a dog, a cat, or anything. This need not be a physical act; it could be internal action. Just do it throughout the day, once an hour. See if it can become once a minute. When it becomes once a minute, there is no need to use your hands and body; simply do it within yourself. Once that becomes your way of being, you are a devotee.

Even if you spend a lifetime, you still won't understand a leaf, an elephant, an ant, or an atom. You are incapable of figuring out even a molecule of DNA. Everything you cannot grasp is in a higher state of existential intelligence than you are. When you see this—really see this—you are a devotee.

A devotee is someone who is willing to dissolve into the object of devotion. If you are a devotee of life, you will become one with it. Don't be an outsider to the life process. Become a devotee. Dissolve.

Energy

Following the Pranic Trail

At present, human beings identify with the body and the mind in a variety of ways. But fundamentally, what you call "myself" is just a certain amount of energy. Modern science has proved beyond all doubt that all of existence is made up of the same energy, manifesting itself in millions of bewilderingly different ways. When Einstein gives us the formula $E = mc^2$, he is, to put it simply, saying that everything in the universe can be seen as just one energy. Religions all over the world have been proclaiming the same thing using somewhat different terminology when they assert that "God is everywhere."

Modern science has arrived at its conclusions through mathematical deduction. Religion has arrived at its conclusions through belief. But the yogi is a hard nut who will not settle for deduction or belief. He or she seeks to *experience* the ultimate through the enhancement of individual perception. Consequently, the yogic tradition does not mention God, or deny it either.

The human longing to expand is actually just an expression of the ultimate formless intelligence that is the very source of who we are. Instead of trying to find the source of our longing, we try to give it expression in the outside world. Due to the nature of our outward-bound senses, we are deceived into believing that outward expression will somehow bring fulfillment. When you misinterpret the expression as the cause, it will only bring entanglement, not freedom.

The sole aim of every individual's life energies is to touch the infinite—the very core of our making. They know no other aim. Your mind may be thinking of money or a new house, your body may be longing for food or sleep, but your life energies are always longing to break the boundaries set by your physical and mental structures. Slowly, in the process of living, many people have stopped following the trajectory of their life energies. The result is that they start believing that they are separate or autonomous entities.

But separateness is a myth. The content of both your physical and mental bodies has been gathered from the outside. They belong to you but they are not you. If you want to go the way your body is going currently, you should know that it is going straight to the grave. Similarly, whatever you know as the mind is a complex mess of all the stuff that it has been accumulating. The objectives of the mind are entirely self-created. They may seem to be fine right now, but they usually take you completely away from the process of life. So, if you go the way your mind goes, you should know you are heading toward an alternative psychological creation; it may be fascinating, stimulating, or even comforting for a length of time, but it bears no relation at all to existential reality.

The entire yogic process is aimed at aligning oneself with the natural longing of life to expand in an unlimited way. It gives conscious expression to this basic human need. The various spiritual practices in the yogic sciences are intended to assist this longing on three levels: the physical body, the mental body, and the third sheath, or layer, of the human mechanism, the *pranamayakosha,* or the energy body.

Yoga means to experience the mental and physical process distinctly, not as the basis of yourself, but as *that which is caused by you.* If you manage these two instruments of body and mind consciously, then your experience of life is one hundred percent of your making. All you need to do is create a distance between you and everything that you accumulated from outside.

Everything that you have gathered in this life accompanies you wherever you go. It is deeply attached to you, and you, in turn, are deeply attached to it, on some unconscious level. It becomes an encumbrance because you don't know when to put it down and when to pick it up. It is like a sack you carry on your shoulders all the time.

But it *is* possible for you to put it down. It will still be your companion, but at least it won't be that burdensome! It is definitely possible to create some distance between you and what you have gathered. You can use it when you want, but you need not be identified with it. If you cannot maintain this distance, your whole vision of life will be clouded. Your memory and your imagination—which includes all your ideas, beliefs, and emotions—belong to the psychological realm. *Life can be tasted and transcended only when there is a distinction between the psychological and the existential.*

The spiritual process means a return to life. It means following the deep intelligence of your life energies. There are

many ways of recognizing which way your life energies want
to go. If you dis-identify with physiological and psychological
processes, you will clearly see this. It is only when you consciously head in the direction of your life energies that you
find equanimity and harmony. It is only in such a stable state
that you would dare to explore the highest levels of exuberance and venture into the deepest mysteries of life.

PAIN NOT SUFFERING

In my motorcycle days, I used to ride all over the country. One day when I was in a remote area, a freak accident occurred, and my calf muscle was slashed right up
to the bone. So I went to a local clinic and asked the
doctor to fix my leg. The doctor examined the wound
and said there was no way he could, because he had no
anesthetic facility. He suggested that I rush to a bigger
hospital and seek immediate medical attention. I said I
didn't have the time, that I had to continue my journey
because I had a schedule to meet. I told him he had to
fix it. He refused. I was bleeding profusely. After much
argument, he gave in because a pool of blood was gath-
ering where I stood. So without any anesthesia, he
began to put my muscle together, which took about
fifty-two sutures on three different levels. Through this
entire process, I was having a conversation with him. He
was sweating and puffing through it all. After it was

over, he asked me incredulously, "Is there no pain in your leg at all?"

There *was* pain. Terrible, unbearable pain. But pain is a natural phenomenon, and it is good. Without it you wouldn't know if your leg was chopped off. But suffering is another matter altogether. Pain is bad enough; why make it worse with suffering? Suffering is entirely self-created. And every human being has the choice: to suffer or not to suffer. It doesn't take much intelligence to choose the latter.

The Karmic Conundrum

Once it happened . . . On a certain day, Shankaran Pillai was sitting in a bar with his buddies. Suddenly, the clock struck eight. Shankaran Pillai put down his glass, rose, and started walking toward the door.

His friends said, "Hey, what's the problem? Where are you going? Why don't you finish your drink?" But Shankaran Pillai kept walking wordlessly, zombielike, toward the door.

The friends laughed and said, "Okay, now we know! It's eight o'clock and you have to be home. You're afraid of your wife, aren't you? What are you—a man or a mouse?"

Shankaran Pillai stopped, turned around, and said, "I am the man of the house. If I were a mouse, my wife would be afraid of me!"

He walked slowly home. His wife's rule was that he should

reach home by eight. Today, the man-mouse argument and his slow, inebriated pace had delayed him. His wife was sitting on the porch, rolling pin in hand. She glowered at him and said, "You fool, once again drinking? Come here and I'll show you."

Shankaran Pillai was a frail but agile man. He walked toward her meekly, but then suddenly leapt over her and ran into the house. She rose and lumbered in after him. He made her run all over the house, confident that she would never be able to catch him. After much running around, he darted into the bedroom and dove under the bed. She rushed behind him. She was a big woman and could not slip under the bed. He lay there, secure, as she hollered, "You coward! What are you doing there under the bed? Come on out! Are you a man or a mouse?"

Shankaran Pillai replied, "I am the man of this house. I have the freedom to lie down wherever I want."

It was the only place he could be at that moment, but he needed to claim it was his freedom! Unfortunately, most human beings are doing much the same thing: they are labeling their compulsions, their limitations, as their choices. If you can joyfully do whatever is needed in a given situation, this is freedom. But limiting yourself to doing only what you like is a horribly compulsive way to live. This compulsiveness is the trick of *karma*—that ancient word that has been mangled by popular usage across the world.

What exactly *is* karma?

"Karma" literally means "action." Action is of three kinds. It could be in terms of the body, mind, or energy. Whatever you do with your body, mind, or energy, leaves a certain residue. This residue forms a pattern of its own, and these resultant patterns stay with you. When you gather a huge volume of impressions, slowly these shape themselves into tendencies, and you become like an automatic toy, a slave to your patterns, a puppet of your past.

Karma is like old software that you have written for yourself, unconsciously. Depending on the type of actions that you perform, you write your software. Once you write a certain type of software, your whole system functions accordingly. Based on the information from the past, certain memory patterns are formed and keep recurring. Now, life is just cyclical.

This is why the same patterns keep returning in your life. There are a few variations, but they remain essentially the same, repeating themselves across generations. After a while, this repetitiveness can be deadly. It is important to see that these patterns rule you from within, not from without. No one has to exercise any external control upon you. Your inner autocrat rules you all the time. You may think it is a new day. Circumstances may change, but internally you are experiencing the same thing over and over again. And so, the more things change, the more they stay the same—not physically but experientially! You are helplessly stuck in the karmic rut.

Freedom is now an empty word because the way you think, feel, and understand life—even the way you sit, stand, and move—is conditioned by your past impressions. From the moment you were born, your parents, your family, your education, your friends, where you lived, and where you traveled—all this decided everything about you. Karma is encrypted on every aspect of life. It is imprinted on your mental memory, the fundamentals of your body, your chemistry, your very energy. These are all backup systems. Even if you lose your body or your mind, you still do not lose your karma! The backup systems are so efficient.

What you consider to be your personality—the bundle of traits and tendencies that you are—is because of information you have gathered unconsciously. These tendencies have been traditionally described as *vasanas*. The word "vasana" literally means "smell." Depending upon what type of garbage is in the bin today, that is the kind of smell that will emanate from it. Depending upon what type of smell you emit, you attract certain kinds of life situations to yourself.

Suppose today there is rotten fish in the garbage bin. It may stink for you, but many other creatures are drawn to it. Tomorrow, if there are flowers in the garbage bin, it smells different and still other creatures are drawn to it.

When I first went down south to the city of Coimbatore almost thirty years ago, I stayed as a guest in a physician's house. He was a gregarious man and told me of an incident that happened in his family. They were from a coastal region in India, and his elder daughter was particularly fond of fish. She was studying up north in the hills of Dehradun where she did not get fish to eat, so whenever she came home for her vacation, she wanted to have it every day. His wife was a vegetarian, but she would cook fish even though she did not eat it.

There is a particular small dried fish that you would know if you are from that part of the country. It has an incredible odor. If it is being carried in a truck, you would like to drive two miles behind the truck or hold your breath as you pass it. Cooking it in the house is a pretty good strategy to evict your neighbors from their home! This girl wanted *that* particular fish to be prepared.

So as they were frying this dried fish, it was as if the entire house was being fumigated. Such an odor could raise the dead! The mother went into the kitchen to tell the cooks how to prepare it, but the moment the stink began to emanate from the frying pan, she ran out of the kitchen because she could not stand it. Meanwhile, the girl, who was in her bedroom, also smelled it and ran out, following the scent. Both mother and daughter crashed headlong into each other—and the mother ended up with a broken nose!

I mention this incident not as an illustration of reward and punishment but as an illustration of the possible consequences of strong attachment and aversion. When these dominate your life, some kind of smashup is inevitable. Vasanas, or tendencies, are generated by a vast accumulation of impressions caused by your physical, mental, and energy actions. What you call your personality is just an expression of these tendencies.

Now, today if you are doing something in a particular way and someone asks you why you can't do it differently, you often declare, "This is my nature. Can't I do what I want?" This is *not* your nature. You are *not* doing what you want. These tendencies have become compulsive. This is your bondage, a kind of software you are writing for yourself unconsciously. Once your software is fixed, it looks as if there is only one path you can walk in your life. It looks as if your destiny is predetermined. A spiritual process, however, means we have made up our minds to rewrite our software, *consciously*.

In India, "karma" is a common word. If people exhibit any kind of compulsive behavior, others will immediately say,

"Oh, that is their karma." This means that it is *of their mak-ing*. The bitterness or sweetness of any experience is not in the event itself, but in how you perceive and respond to it. What is a very bitter experience for one person could be a blessing for another.

Once a grief-stricken man sat by a gravestone, crying bit-terly and hitting his head against it. "My life! Oh, how sense-less it is. My body is a worthless carcass now that you have gone. If only you had lived! If only fate had not been so cruel! If only you hadn't left, how different my life would have been!"

A clergyman nearby overheard him and said, "I assume the person lying beneath this mound of earth was someone of great importance to you?"

"Importance? Yes, indeed!" wept the man, wailing even louder. "It was my wife's first husband!"

So, the quality of your life is always decided by *how* you experience life, not by *what* life offers you.

It is important to remember that karma is not a negative word. Karma is what gives stability and structure to your life. Every moment, impressions are flooding in torrents into your system through your five sense organs and each of them is being recorded. There is nothing wrong with this stored infor-mation. It is very useful for your survival. If you deleted all of it, you would not know how to handle even the simplest as-pects of life. The spiritual process does not seek to demolish this storehouse of karmic impressions, but helps you to be-come more conscious of it, and establish a little space, which allows you to stand outside of it.

So, your software is not in itself the problem. It turns into a problem only if it becomes the ruling factor in your life. To talk of good karma and bad karma is like talking of good bondage and bad bondage. There is no such thing. Karma is just your own creation. It is neither good nor bad. It is software that can be useful if you have some freedom from it. This is all the spiritual process aims to do: loosen the grip of karma upon you. Whatever be the nature of your past karma, there is enough awareness in a human being to take complete charge of the karma of the present moment.

If you want any kind of transformation, any kind of forward movement in your life, it can only happen if you break the cyclical patterns of karma. Anything that is cyclical suggests constant motion, but it doesn't really go anywhere. If you are sensitive to life, you realize this early. If you are less sensitive, you realize this as you grow older. Everything may seem to be going your way: your professional life may be flourishing, your capital may be increasing, your family may be thriving, but *you* are not really getting anywhere. The faster you achieve your success, the faster you realize this. When you are in a certain state of insufficiency, you keep thinking that everything will be okay once your dreams are realized. But if all the things you dreamt of happen very quickly, you suddenly realize that, although everything is happening as you thought it should, life still remains unfulfilled and your longings persist.

Until you break this cycle, there is no real choice in your life. Sometimes, you may have felt you have experienced a breakthrough. Things seem to have changed, and everything seems great for the next three days, but on the fourth day, you fall back into the same rut. Hasn't this happened to you any number of times? That is because there is no freedom of thought, emotion, action, and, above all, no freedom of experience as long as you are in the karmic grip.

At the same time, avoiding karma is not the answer either. Avoidance may give you some balance and stability in day-to-day life, but slowly it saps you of life and joy. This is very negative karma in itself. Denying, suppressing, or avoiding life brings more bondage than freedom. The desire, "I don't want karma," is itself a big karma!

The very process of living is itself a dissolution of karma. If you live every moment of your life totally, you dissolve enormous amounts of karma. When you experience everything that comes your way absolutely, when you experience every life breath with utmost intensity, without the distractions of thought and emotion, devoid of any psychological drama, you are liberated from the very process of birth and death. You are not only more alive; you *are* life itself.

Yoga offers a way to distance yourself not just from your karma, but from the very source of karma, which is the discriminatory intellect. It offers you the choice every moment of your existence to be either a victim or a spectator or the very master of your life. With a certain amount of effort and practice we all can write a software of joy and well-being for ourselves.

Sadhana

—∞∞∞—

When you realize that all your material achievements are of value only in comparison with those who don't have them, this is joy that springs from another's deprivation. Can you really call this joy? Isn't it actually a kind of sickness? It is time everyone addressed this. If you were alone on this planet, what would you want for yourself? Ask yourself this question and see where it takes you.

Try this. Sit alone for five minutes and see what your life would be like if you were absolutely alone in this world. If there were nobody or nothing to compare yourself with, what would you truly long for? What would really matter to you if there were no external appreciation or critique? If you do this every day, you will become aligned with the longings of the life that you are, rather than the accumulated karmic mess that you believe you are.

The Mechanics of Life

Fundamentally, *kriya* means "internal action." An internal action is one that does not involve either the body or the mind or the physical dimensions of energy. As we have established earlier, the body and the mind are yours, but still external to you. You have gathered both from the outside: the body is an accumulation of food, and the mind an accumulation of ideas. Even the imprints upon the energy body are an accumulation of the impressions of the five senses. When you have the ability to perform action with the *non-physical aspect of your energy*, then it is termed a "kriya." All this may sound somewhat esoteric, but only if you are inducted by someone who has mastery over the realms of energy will it become possible for you to practice a kriya.

If your actions find outward expression, involving body, mind, and the physical dimensions of energy, that is karma. But if you turn inward and perform an action beyond all dimensions of physicality, that is kriya. Karma is the process of binding you. Kriya is the process of liberating you. The most significant aspect of yoga is always to perform action beyond the physical dimensions of energy. Among the four dimensions of physicality, you are most conscious of bodily actions, less of the mental, much less of the emotional, and negligibly of the energetic. The moment you learn to perform action with the non-physical aspect of your life energy, you suddenly move to a new level of freedom within and outside of yourself.

How do you access the non-physical aspect of your life energy? The yogic practices, which involve postures, breath, attitudes of the mind, and energy activation, are all essentially oriented toward aligning the first three layers of the body: the physical, the mental, and the energetic body. It is only in aligning them that you find access to dimensions beyond the physical—to the fundamental life energy itself.

I have seen any number of people who start doing a simple kriya, and suddenly become so creative that they are able to achieve things that they never imagined possible in their lives. This is simply because they loosened their karmic foundations a little. They shook up their life energies for a change, instead of being entangled with their physical processes of body, mind, and energy. This is something every human being can learn to do.

Kriya yoga is a very powerful way to walk the spiritual path, but at the same time it is tremendously demanding. For many modern urban people who are unaccustomed to using their body in its full versatility, kriya yoga could seem arduous and inhuman. This is because kriyas are elaborate and involve a great deal of discipline, focus, and exactitude. Most people do not have the body, the attitude, or the stability of emotion for this yoga path, primarily because they are used to living, right from their childhood, in a perpetual state of comfort. Being used to a level of physical comfort is not a problem. But being in constant quest of comfort: this is a great problem. That kind of attitude and emotion is unsuitable for the path of kriya yoga.

Also, kriya yoga cannot be done with people who talk "freedom" all the time. It is not for people who keep asking, "Why am I not free to eat my ice cream? Why can't I wake up whenever I feel like it? Why can't I eat, drink, or have sex with whatever, whoever, whenever I feel like?" If you take the path of kriya, a certain fundamental discipline has to be brought into all physical, psychological, and emotional processes. If you want to hit the peak of your consciousness, this discipline is essential. You cannot be partying till early morning and attempt to scale Mount Everest tomorrow! The same logic holds true here.

When you are given a certain kriya yoga regimen, you have to follow it. You may understand the need for the discipline as you go along, but it can never be fully explained. And if it has to be explained, the essence of the kriya will be lost. This is because kriya is a tool to transcend the framework of logic and experience in order to access those non-physical dimensions that are considered spiritual or mystical.

If I wanted to teach you kriyas just as practices, it would be simple to put them in a book from which you could learn and memorize them. But for the kriya to be a live process, to be imprinted in your system in a certain way, it needs a certain discipline, dedication, and receptivity. When you walk a completely new terrain, if there is no trust in the one who guides you, then the journey becomes unnecessarily long and difficult.

Generally, on the path of kriya, most gurus make the disciples wait. Traditionally, when students went to a guru to learn kriya yoga, they might well have been told to sweep the floor for a year, and then wash the dishes for another! If their trust still did not waver, then the guru might consider initiating them into the kriyas. There is a reason for this. Once you empower people in a particular way that makes their system vibrant beyond normal standards, they can cause great damage to themselves if their attitudes and emotions are not as they should be. But in today's world, to get that kind of time with people, to arrive at that kind of trust and then imprint these kriyas, is difficult. It is not impossible, but the chances are remote.

I spent twenty-one years of my life transforming a powerful kriya, the *Shambhavi Mahamudra,* in order that it might be taught to large numbers of people in today's world. Certain aspects that could empower people either to harm themselves or others, or influence the elements around them have been firewalled, so only the physical, psychological, and spiritual benefits remain. For those two decades I deliberately stayed away from all forms of public outreach, because my entire focus was primarily on re-crafting the kriya to ensure that it could be widely imparted without any adverse effects.

Kriya yoga as a full-fledged path is important only for those interested in exploring mystical dimensions. If your concern is only well-being or if you are just seeking realization, kriyas can be used in a small way. But kriya yoga as an exclusive path is not necessary because it requires too much application.

If you follow the path of kriya very intensely without guidance, it may take a few lifetimes to bear fruit. If you have someone to actively guide the process, kriya can be a most powerful and magnificent way to explore the inner nature and mystical phenomena. Otherwise kriya is a somewhat roundabout route. What you are seeking on this path is not just well-being, blissfulness, or realization. Instead, you want to know the very mechanics of life-making; you want to know the engineering of life. That is why it is a much longer process.

People on the kriya path have a completely different kind of presence about them because of the mastery over their energies. They can dismantle life and put it back together. If you are pursuing the path of gnana, for example, your intellect could become razor-sharp, but there is still very little you can do with your energies. Similarly, on the path of bhakti, or devotion, there is nothing much you can do with your energies. (Nor do you care, because the intense sweetness of your emotions is all that matters; you only want to dissolve into the object of your devotion.) If you are on the path of karma, you can do many things in the external world, but you can do nothing with yourself. Kriya yogis, on the other hand, can do whatever they wish with their inner world, and achieve a great deal in the outer world as well.

Sadhana

The very way the karmic structure works in every human being is essentially cyclical. If you observe very closely, within a day the same cycles are happening many times over. If you are very observant, you will see that every forty minutes you are going through a physiological cycle. Once you see that, then with the necessary attention and awareness you can ride the cycle and move toward transcendence from the limitations that these cycles set. So, every forty minutes, life presents you with an opportunity—the opportunity to become conscious.

Every forty to forty-eight minutes, there is also a shift of dominance in the way the breath is moving through the right and left nostrils. It is dominant in the right nostril for a length of time, and then in the left. Become aware of this so you know at least something about you is changing. This awareness can be further enhanced into awareness of the solar and lunar influences upon the body. If you bring your physical system in sync with the lunar and solar cycles, your physical and psychological health is guaranteed.

The Energy Labyrinth

The yogic system offers us a comprehensive and elaborate view of the anatomy of the human energy body. It has mapped seventy-two thousand channels (or *nadis*, as they are called) in the energy system. The *prana*, or energy, moves through these channels. These seventy-two thousand channels spring, in turn, from three basic channels. The channel on the right is known as *pingala,* the left is known as *ida,* and the central is known as *sushumna.*

These three channels are the basis of the energy system. Pingala is symbolized as the masculine and ida is symbolized as the feminine. "Masculine" and "feminine" do not refer here to biological differences, but to certain qualities in nature that have been identified as such. These qualities are represented by these two channels.

If a person's pingala is very pronounced, then outgoing, exploratory qualities will be dominant. If the ida is more pronounced, receptive and reflective qualities will be dominant. Whether one is a man or woman has nothing to do with this. You may be a man, but the ida may be more dominant; you may be a woman, but the pingala may be more dominant.

The pingala and ida are also symbolized as the sun and the moon—the sun representing the masculine, and moon representing the feminine. The sun is aggressive and outgoing; the moon receives and reflects. The cycles of the moon are deeply connected with the female body as well. On the level of your mind, pingala represents the logical dimension; ida represents the intuitive dimension. These two dualities are the fundamentals of the physical sphere of life. A human being is complete only when both the masculine and the feminine function at full force and are in proper balance.

Sushumna, the central nadi, is the most significant aspect of your physiology, yet it generally goes unexplored. It is independent of the seventy-two thousand nadis, but it is the fulcrum of the whole system. Once the energies enter your sushumna, irrespective of what is happening around you, you have a certain balance. Right now, you may be reasonably balanced, but if the outside situation is challenging, you will also be disturbed. Once energies enter the sushumna, however, your inner way of being becomes independent of the outside, because it is independent of the seventy-two thousand nadis.

There is a great deal of *chakra* talk nowadays. "Chakra" means "wheel," and has a very specific meaning and significance in the yogic system. These days there are "wheel alignment centers" that claim to balance your chakras, clear your blocks, and heal you of ailments, past, present, and future. Lots of people are "doing" chakras these days. It has become a huge fad, but it can be dangerous. It is time to approach this very subtle subject with care and precision.

The nadis do not have a physical manifestation. If you cut the body and look inside, you will not find them. But as you become more aware, you will notice the energy is not moving at random but in established pathways.

The chakras are powerful centers in the physiology where the nadis meet in a particular way to create an energy vortex. Like the nadis, the chakras are of a subtle nature and do not have a physical existence. They always meet in the form of a triangle (not a circle, as the word "chakra" suggests). The moving part in a machine is always a circle, because a circle is capable of movement with least resistance. These energy centers are so named because the wheel suggests movement or dynamism.

There are 114 chakras in the body. Two are outside the body and 112 are within the body. Among these 112, there are

7 major chakras. For most people, 3 of these are active; the remaining are either dormant or mildly active. You do not have to activate all 114 chakras to live a physical life. You can live quite a complete life with just a few of them. If you were to activate all 114 chakras, you would have no sense of body at all. The purpose of yoga is to activate your energy system in such a way that your body consciousness is constantly being lowered, so you can sit here *in* the body, but *are* no longer the body.

In southern India, there was a legendary yogi named Sadashiva Brahmendra. He was a *nirkaya,* which literally means "bodiless yogi." He had no sense of body. Wearing clothes does not even occur to a person in such a state. He just walked around naked. Also in such a condition, there is no sense of home, property, or physical boundary.

One day, he happened to walk into the king's garden on the banks of the river Kaveri. The king was sitting there, relaxing with his queens. Sadashiva Brahmendra wandered into the garden, unaware of his own nakedness. The king was furious. "Who is this fool that dares to walk naked in front of my women?"

He sent his soldiers after him. The soldiers ran behind Sadashiva Brahmendra, calling out to him. He did not turn back. He continued to walk. Angered, one of the soldiers took out his sword and struck him, severing his right arm. Sadashiva Brahmendra did not even break his stride. He continued walking.

Seeing this, the soldiers were wonderstruck and terrified. They realized that this was no ordinary man. The king and his soldiers ran after him, prostrated, begged his forgiveness, and brought him back to the garden. He lived in that garden for the rest of his life, and finally shed his body there.

There are innumerable instances like this in the yogic tradition. When your energies are in a heightened condition, the sense of the physical is so diminished that it is even possible to go without any external nourishment for days on end.

What exactly is the role of the chakras within the system?

There are seven fundamental chakras: the *muladhara,* which is located at the perineum, the space between the anal outlet and the genital organ; *swadhishthana,* which is just above the genital organ; *manipuraka,* which is three fourths of an inch below the navel; *anahata,* which is below the point where the rib cage meets the diaphragm; *vishuddhi,* which is at the pit of the throat; *agna,* which is between the eyebrows; and *sahasrara,* also known as the *brahmarandra,* which is at the fontanel on top of the head (where newborn infants have a soft spot).

The chakras are the seven different dimensions through which your energies find expression. Experiences that happen within you—anger, misery, peace, joy, and ecstasy—are different levels of expression of your life energies. If your energies are dominant in muladhara, then food and sleep will be the most dominant factors in your life. If your energies are dominant in swadhishthana, pleasure will be most dominant in your life; this means you enjoy your physical reality in many ways. If your energies are dominant in manipuraka, you are a doer; you can accomplish many things in the world. If your energies are dominant in anahata, you are a very creative person. If your energies are dominant in vishuddhi, you will develop a powerful presence. If your energies are dominant in agna, then you are intellectually realized. Intellectual realization can bring you to a certain state of peace and stability within yourself, irrespective of what is happening outside of you.

These are just different levels of intensity. A pleasure-seeker has more intensity to his life than someone whose life is just food and sleep. The man who wants to initiate something in the world has much more intensity than a pleasure-seeker. An artist or a creative person lives his life more intensely compared to these three people. If you move into vishuddhi, it is a completely different dimension of intensity and agna is higher still. If you hit your sahasrara, you will explode into unexplained ecstasies. Without any external stimulant or reason, you are simply ecstatic because your energies have touched a certain peak.

It is misleading to speak of lower and higher chakras. It is like comparing the foundation of the building to the roof. The roof is not superior; the foundation is not inferior. The quality, life span, stability, and security of a building depend, to a large extent, more on the foundation than on the roof. For example, in the physical body, your energies need to be in the *muladhara* chakra to some extent. "Mula" means the root or source, and "adhara" means foundation. In the engineering of the body, this is the base. If you wish to grow, you need to cultivate this.

At the same time, chakras have a spiritual dimension, not just a physical one. If you bring the right amount of awareness to it, the same muladhara can be transformed to a point where you become absolutely free of the compulsive need for food and sleep.

The chakras fall into one of two different dimensions: the muladhara, swadhishthana, manipuraka, and related chakras are more concerned with keeping the body stable and rooted. These are qualities associated with the earth, with self-preservation. When your energies are dominant in these chakras, your qualities are earthy and you are more in the grip of nature. The upper chakras—the vishuddhi, agna, sahasrara, and related chakras—are centers that draw you away from the pull of the earth. They are concerned with the longing for the infinite. They make you receptive to a force that we customarily refer to as grace.

The middle chakra, anahata, is a balance between the two. It is like a transition between your lower and upper chakras, between survival instincts and the instinct toward liberation. It is symbolized by two interlocking triangles, one pointing downward and another upward, forming a six-pointed star. Many religious traditions have used the star as a sacred symbol, because some enlightened beings in these cultures realized their original nature through the anahata, and discovered the interlocking triangles of this chakra within themselves.

The vishuddhi chakra, located in the pit of your throat, literally means "filter." If your vishuddhi becomes powerful, you have the ability to filter everything that enters you. Or in other words, once your vishuddhi is very active, you grow so powerful that external nature has no influence over you. Indian iconography depicts Adiyogi, or Shiva, with a blue throat, because he is capable of filtering all the poisons of the outside world and preventing them from entering his system by stalling them in his throat.

If your energies move into the agna chakra, located between your eyebrows, you are intellectually enlightened, but still not experientially liberated. The great mystic philosopher of eighth-century India Adi Shankara walked all across the land, defeating legions of scholars in metaphysical debate. His logic was unbeatable, because the union experienced in agna endows one with an extraordinary level of intellectual insight and perception.

The seventh chakra, sahasrara, is actually located just outside the body. For most people, it is dormant. Through spiritual practice or a very intense way of living, you can activate this. If you hit your sahasrara, your experience is no longer intellectual; it is experiential. You now explode into unexplained ecstasies and the deepest mystical realms start opening up. Sometimes you can attain ecstasies that can turn uncontrollable, if there is not sufficient spiritual practice to create the necessary physiological and psychological balance. In the Indian tradition, these ecstatic mystics were termed *avadhutas*. They were in such altered states of consciousness that they often had to be fed and taken care of by those around them because they were incapable of handling the worldly aspects of life on their own.

Fundamentally, any spiritual path can be described as the journey from the muladhara to the sahasrara, an evolution from one dimension to another. There is a wide spectrum of spiritual practices in the yogic system that enables one to move one's energies from one chakra to another. However, from the agna to the sahasrara, there is no path. You have either to leap or fall into it.

This is one of the reasons for the tremendous emphasis on the guru in the Indian spiritual tradition. To make the leap from the agna to the sahasrara takes immense trust. Suppose you were confronted by a bottomless abyss, and someone asked you to plunge into it, you would either have to be utterly crazy, extraordinarily courageous, or absolutely trusting to do it. Almost no one has the kind of courage it takes. Very few are mad enough to live their lives with total abandon; most people live with caution and the overriding need to protect their boundaries. So, for 99.9 percent of the people, what is needed is trust. Without trust, they will never make the leap.

However, the abyss need not conjure dark images of a terrifying pit. Instead, it signifies a space free of all possibility of hurt and suffering, an entirely new dimension that is flawlessly non-repetitive, a dimension beyond comparison and context that leaves you not as an individual but as all-encompassing infinite nature, in a stillness beyond bliss.

And so, the leap is worth it. The leap is everything. With the leap, the bottomless abyss becomes boundless freedom.

Sadhana

By focusing at a point six to nine inches away from the region between your eyebrows for twelve to forty-eight minutes, with your eyes open, you can realize the nature and structure of your individual chakras (depending on the duration and your level of focus). This perception can help in stabilizing the random movement of chakras in the human physiology due to stressful external situations. This is just one aspect of a very sophisticated form of kriya yoga that allows you access to your inner akashic, or etheric, dimension.

UNCHARTED PATH

The sixth limb of yoga is referred to as *dhyana*, or *dhyan*, which is essentially about transcending the boundaries of one's physical and mental framework. Dhyan traveled from India to China along with the Buddhist monks, where it was referred to as *Ch'an*. This yoga traveled through the Southeast Asian countries to Japan and became *Zen*, and found expression as a whole system of direct insight without an emphasis on doctrine. Zen is a spiritual path that has no scriptures, books, rules, or rigid practices; it is an uncharted path.

The first recorded use of the method we now call Zen happened almost eight thousand years ago, well before the time of Gautama the Buddha. King Janaka was a brilliant man and ardent seeker, burning with the longing to know. He had exhausted all the spiritual teachers in the kingdom. None of them could help him because they were all born out of the book. He had still to meet someone who came from inner experience.

One day the king went on a hunting trip. Riding deep into the jungle, he caught sight of a yogi. He stopped. Seated outside a small hermitage was Ashtavakra, one of the most accomplished yogis and spiritual masters of all time. Janaka prepared to get off the horse to greet him. He swung his leg over the saddle and was about to dismount when Ashtavakra said, "Stop!"

So, Janaka stopped right there, one leg still in the stirrup and the other midair. It was a painful position to be in, but Janaka stayed frozen, staring at Ashtavakra. We don't know how long the guru held him that way, but suddenly in that awkward state, Janaka became fully enlightened. The method employed by Ashtavakra was akin to what is generally known in the world as Zen today.

Once it happened . . . There was a Zen master whom everyone respected, but who had no teaching to impart. He always carried a huge sack on his shoulders; this would contain many items, and some of it would be sweets. In every town and village that he visited, children would gather around him, and he would distribute sweets and leave. People asked for teachings, but he would just laugh and go on his way.

One day, a man who was himself known to be a Zen master of great repute, came to meet him. He wanted to ascertain whether this man with a sack was really in Zen or not. So he asked him, "What is Zen?" Immediately, the man dropped the sack and stood straight.

Then he asked, "What is the goal of Zen?" The man picked up the sack, slung it over his shoulders, and walked away.

This is what yoga is also about. This is what every spiritual practice is about. When you want to attain yoga or Zen, you have to drop your load, discard everything on the way, remain free, stand upright. It is important. With your load, you may never do it. And what is the goal of yoga? Consciously take on the whole load once again. And now it no longer feels like a load!

Sacred Science

What does it mean to sanctify or consecrate a space?

The word "consecration" is often used somewhat loosely. For most people, it denotes a series of rituals that offers, at best, beauty and poetry to our lives, but performs no real useful function. Most believe it is mere mumbo jumbo meant to obfuscate the spiritual process and exploit a fearful and gullible majority. It is time to discard this superficial understanding and look deeper.

If you transform mud into food, we call this agriculture. If you make food into flesh and bone, we call this digestion. If you make flesh into mud, we call this cremation. If you make this flesh, or even a stone or empty space, into a higher possibility, this is consecration.

Consecration is a live process. The Sanskrit word for it is *pratishtha*. As we have discussed earlier, modern science today tells us that everything is the same energy manifesting itself in a million different ways. If that is so, what you call the divine, what you call a stone, what you call a man or a woman, or a demon, are all the same energy functioning in different ways. If you have the necessary technology, you can make the simple space around you into a divine exuberance. You can just take a piece of rock and make it into a god or a goddess. This is the phenomenon of consecration.

An enormous amount of knowledge about consecration has been perpetuated across generations since ancient times, particularly in India. This is because regardless of how good your life is, or how long you live, at some point the fundamental human longing to get in touch with the source of creation will invariably assert itself. If the possibility to access these deeper dimensions is not created and made available to every individual who seeks, then society has failed to provide authentic well-being for its citizens.

It is because of this awareness that the Indian culture built numerous temples on every street. The idea was not to create temples that were in competition with one another. The idea was simply that no one should live in a space that is not consecrated.

It is tremendous good fortune for a human being to live in a consecrated space. When you do, the very way you live becomes distinctly different. You may ask, "Can't I live without it?" You can. If you know how to make your very body into a temple, going to the temple is not so significant. Yes, you can consecrate your own body. But the question is, are you able to keep it that way?

All spiritual initiations have been aimed at consecrating this very flesh into a temple-like space. After that, all that is needed is maintenance. Doing a spiritual practice every day is one way of trying to maintain the human system in a high state of vibrancy after an initiation. I have given powerful consecrations to people at various times, sometimes formally, sometimes informally. To consecrate an inanimate object—a rock, for example—costs an enormous amount of life. Making human beings into living temples is much more inexpensive and eco-friendly—and besides, they are mobile! There are many advantages, but the problem is human beings have to dedicate a certain amount of time, energy, and focus to maintenance, otherwise it will not work.

When people in the world are too distracted and unwilling to make themselves into living temples, building stone temples becomes a necessity. The basic purpose of building a temple is to benefit the majority of people who have no spiritual practice in their lives. If one can do some spiritual practice in such a consecrated space, it is doubly beneficial. Particularly for those who do not know how to make their own body into a temple, the outer temple is invaluable.

Consecration, or pratishtha, is done in various ways, but generally by using rituals, mantras, sounds, forms, and various other ingredients. Constant maintenance is required. The rituals in the temples are not for your sake; they are to keep the deity or energy form alive. What is a deity? A deity is a tool for a specific purpose: to achieve fulfillment in different aspects of life. In fact, the traditional word for deity is *yantra*, which literally translates as machine or a working energy form. Traditional wisdom has always advised people against keeping stone idols at home. If you keep them, you must maintain them every day with the right kind of processes. If a deity is consecrated through mantras, and if the necessary maintenance does not happen on a daily basis, the deity becomes a withdrawing energy and can cause immense harm to people who live in the vicinity. Unfortunately, many temples have become like this because of improper maintenance by people who do not know how to keep them alive.

Prana pratishtha is different in that it uses your own life energies to consecrate something. When you consecrate a form in this way, it does not need any maintenance. It is quite literally forever. When I fulfilled my life mission, which was the consecration of the Dhyanalinga (a subtle energy form with all chakras operating at their optimal capacity, at the Isha Yoga Center in Coimbatore, in southern India, in 1999), it was through prana pratishtha. This is why there are no rituals in this shrine. None are required. The Dhyanalinga does not need any maintenance because its vibrancy will never fluctuate. Even if you take away the stone part of the structure, it will remain the same. Irrespective of physical changes that may happen over time, the energy form will not perish! This is because the real form is made of a non-physical dimension. It is indestructible.

The Indian temples were never places of prayer. The tradition was that you had a shower first thing in the morning and went directly to the temple, sat there for a while, and only then began your day. The temple was like a public battery-charging space. Most people have forgotten this nowadays. They just go to temples, ask for something, bum-bounce on the temple floor, and then leave. This is quite pointless. The idea is to sit and imbibe the energies of the place.

At the Dhyanalinga Yogic Temple in Coimbatore, you are not required to "believe" in anything to reap its benefits. You are not required to pray, or make any ritual offering. You are encouraged to just close your eyes and be in the space for some time. If you were to try it for yourself, you would discover that it is a tremendous experience. The Dhyanalinga is in the highest level of intensity that any form can be. Even if those who do not know anything about meditation come and sit there, they become meditative by their own nature. That is the kind of remarkable tool it is.

If I were given the necessary support and opportunity, I would like to consecrate the whole planet! This is what I am good at: turning thin air into a very powerful vibrant space, turning a piece of metal or stone into a divine reverberation. It is my dream that someday all of humanity should live in a consecrated environment. Your home should be consecrated; your street should be consecrated; your office should be consecrated. All the places where you spend your time should be consecrated. When you live in such a space, your evolution need not stick to the Darwinian scale; you can simply leapfrog ahead to a state of ultimate well-being and freedom.

In India, most ancient temples were built for Shiva, or "that which is not." There are thousands of Shiva temples in the country, and most of them do not have any idol as such. They generally have a representative form, a *linga*.

The word "linga" means "the form." When creation began to happen, or when the unmanifest became manifest, the first form that it assumed was that of an ellipsoid, or a three-dimensional ellipse, which is what we call a linga. It started as an ellipsoid, and then took on many other shapes and forms. If you go into deep states of meditativeness, you will find that before a point of absolute dissolution, once again the energy takes on the form of a linga. Modern cosmologists have identified that the core of every galaxy is always an ellipsoid.

So, generally in yoga, the linga is considered to be the perfect and fundamental form in existence. It is the first form and the final form. In the space between, creation takes place. What lies beyond is "that which is not" or shi-va. So, the linga form is actually an opening in the fabric of creation. For physical creation, the front door is a linga and the back door is a linga! This makes the temple an opening in the fabric of the physical. You could fall right through it and go beyond: that is what makes it such a tremendous possibility.

Interestingly, lingas are found all over the world. In Africa, there are terra-cotta lingas, largely used for occult purposes. In Delphi, Greece, there is a linga below the ground, known as the "navel of the earth." This is purely a manipura linga, meant to promote prosperity and material well-being. When someone showed me a picture of it, I immediately knew what type of people had consecrated this. It was definitely done by Indian yogis thousands of years ago; there is no doubt about that.

When I consecrated Adiyogi: The Abode of Yoga in Tennessee in the year 2015, it was an event of considerable spiritual import—in fact, a milestone for classical yoga in the Western world. Having seen various ancient sites of interest, I am quite certain nothing of this kind of energetic significance has happened in North America, or indeed in the western hemisphere in the last three thousand years. Consecrated through the process of prana pratishtha, the space is a tribute to Adiyogi, the world's first yogi. Exclusively dedicated to the pursuit and practice of yoga, the space represents a living repository of the highest level of energetic vibrancy and exuberance, and offers a unique spiritual possibility to seekers in the West.

Most of the lingas in India right now represent one chakra or two at the most. They are invariably consecrated for material well-being. There are some anahata lingas consecrated to promote peace and joy as well. The uniqueness of the Dhyanalinga is that it has all seven chakras energized at their peak. To create seven separate lingas for seven chakras would have been so much easier, but the impact would not have been the same. So, the Dhyanalinga is like the energy body of the most evolved being, referred to in the yogic culture as "Shiva," eternally available to all. It is the highest possible manifestation.

If you push energy up to very high levels of intensity, it can hold form only until a certain point. Beyond that, it becomes formless and people are largely incapable of experiencing it. The Dhyanalinga has been consecrated in such a way that the energy has been crystallized at the highest point beyond which there can be no form. It was created so that the intimacy of sitting with a live guru is available to every seeker who longs for it.

Above all, what makes the Dhyanalinga an immense and unprecedented spiritual possibility is the fact that it represents the opportunity to experience life in its complete depth and totality. One who comes into its sphere is influenced on the level of the akashic, or etheric body, or the vignanamayakosha. If you bring about a certain transformation through the physical, mental, or energy body, it can be lost in the course of life. But once you are touched on the level of the etheric body, it is forever. Even if you go through many lifetimes, this seed of liberation will wait for the right opportunity to sprout and flower.

It took me three and a half years of a very intense process of consecration to complete the Dhyanalinga. Many yogis and adepts have attempted to create such a linga, but for various reasons, all the required ingredients never came together. This was not my will; it was my guru's. Though my contact with my master was momentary, it has in every way been momentous. It has directed every step of my life, including my very birth. The Dhyanalinga has finally been accomplished, with his grace and with the love, support, and understanding of many people, who gave themselves, knowingly or unknowingly, willingly or unwillingly, consciously or unconsciously. I am grateful to them all.

Sadhana

If you learn how to use the five elements in a certain simple geometric formation, you can create a highly beneficial energy space for yourself. Here's a simple exercise you can try.

Draw a figure like the one below with rice flour or some kind of grain. Place a small ghee, or clarified butter, lamp in a plate full of water at the center. Place a flower in the water. You have now created a geometric form, using water, fire, and air. The flower in the water represents the earth. Akash, or ether, is, of course, always present.

Try this simple process every evening. You will find the energy of your room altered in a subtle but powerful way. In this manner, you can uniquely empower your home or office on a daily basis.

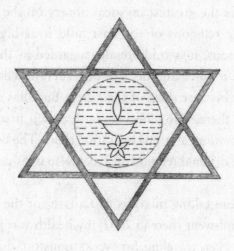

Mountains of Grace

For most yogis and mystics, the problem has been that they could never share the fruits of their realization with people around them. To find another person capable of receiving what you know is not easy. If you find even one person you are fortunate.

So, most spiritual masters downloaded their knowing in remote but not entirely inaccessible places. They often chose mountain peaks because there is less human traffic and disturbance in such places. There are many wonderful places like this in India. Mount Kailash (the mountain peak in western Tibet that is regarded as a sacred place of immeasurable power and antiquity) is the place where the maximum amount of knowledge has been stored for a very long time in energy form.

Kailash is the greatest mystical library on the planet. Almost all the religions of the East hold it as highly sacred. Among Hindus, it is traditionally regarded as the abode of the great god Shiva and his consort, Parvati. The Buddhists hold it holy because three of their great Buddhas are believed to be living there. The Jains believe that their first great master, or *tirthankara*, attained liberation there. The Bon religion, which is the original religion of Tibet, also considers it deeply sacred.

I have been taking pilgrims to Kailash for the past eleven years. When I went there in 2007, my health was particularly bad. I had been traveling for weeks nonstop, during which baffled medics in different parts of the world had diagnosed me with a variety of illnesses, including malaria, dengue, typhoid, and even cancer. The confounded doctors termed my blood reports "esoteric"! Finally, I decided to look inward and work on myself. A few days later, I went to Kailash. I was better at this point, but still very weak. When I looked at the mountain, I saw there was so much mystical knowledge waiting to be accessed. So I took a strand of energy from the mountain and connected it to my energy system in a certain way. As soon as I did that, there was a sudden resurgence of vitality, and my depleted energy body (ravaged by nearly eight weeks of fever) bounced back to normal. I looked younger, felt younger, and even my voice had changed—just in about an hour's time! The results were visible. There were almost two hundred people around me who witnessed this.

There are other places of enormous vibrational energy where mystics have bequeathed the fruits of their spiritual practice. Such spaces are innumerable in the Himalayas. A variety of mystics and yogis chose these mountains as their abode. When they lived there they naturally left behind a certain dimension of energy, and as a result, the Himalayas gathered a kind of aura.

For example, Kedarnath is just a small temple in the Himalayas. There is no deity there; it is just an outcrop of a rock. But it is one of the most powerful places in the world! If you strive to improve your receptivity and then visit a place like that, it will just blow you away. There are many places like that in the East, but the Himalayas attract the most people.

There is another place called Kumara Parvat in the South Indian state of Karnataka. *Parvat* means "mountain." *Kumara* refers to the son of Shiva, whose name was Kartikeya. He fought many battles, trying to transform the world, but when he realized the futility of this, he came to this region. It is here that he washed his sword of its blood for the last time. He decided that even if he fought for a thousand years, he was never going to change the world; that one violent solution would breed another ten problems. So he climbed up the mountain and stood on the summit. Normally when a yogi wants to shed his body, he will either sit or lie down. But because he was such a warrior, Kartikeya stood up and exited his body, standing.

If one can exit the physical form voluntarily without damaging it, that is an indication of absolute mastery over the life process. This is generally referred to in the Indian tradition as *mahasamadhi,* or "glorious equanimity."

When I went to Kumara Parvat many years ago, a small tent was set up for me. I wanted to sleep in it, but when I went in and tried to lie down, my body would involuntarily move into a standing posture, dismantling the tent. The whole night I was not able to sit; my body would only stand. That is when I started seeing what Kartikeya's life was all about. Although he lived thousands of years ago, what he left behind is still vibrantly alive.

This kind of work can never be wiped out. Wherever a person does something with his life energies, he creates a certain possibility which cannot be erased by any event. The work and presence of anybody who experimented even a little bit with the inner dimensions can never be destroyed.

For example, Gautama the Buddha is supposed to have lived 2,500 years ago, and Jesus is supposed to have lived 2,000 years ago, but as far as I am concerned, both are a living reality. Once you create a certain volume of work with your life energies, it is permanent for all practical purposes and time does not destroy it. If you work with the physical body of flesh and blood, it has a limited life span. If you use your mind, the life span of that work is much longer. But if you work with your fundamental life energies, then the result is timeless.

THE SILVER PEAKS

Ever since my infancy, there was always a certain mountain peak in the background of my gaze. Only when I was sixteen years old and discussed this with my friends (who responded, "You're crazy! Where are mountains?") did I realize that nobody else had mountains in their eyes! For some time I thought I should locate that peak, but then I put the idea aside.

Suppose there were a spot on your spectacles. You'd get used to it after a while. It was just like that with my mountain peak. It was only much later when a flood of memory returned to me, and when I was looking for a place to establish the Dhyanalinga, that I began to search for the peak that had dominated my vision.

I traveled everywhere. I made the 760-mile ride from Goa to Kanyakumari on the southernmost tip of India about eleven times. Along every road and mud track, I have probably ridden thousands of miles.

Then just by chance one day, many years later, I came upon a village outside Coimbatore. As I was driving round a bend, I saw the Seventh Hill of the Velliangiri Mountains. There it was: the mountain that I had seen since my childhood. The moment I set my eyes upon that peak—one that had lived within me for my entire life—it vanished from my inner vision and became a living reality. Suddenly I knew this would be the most conducive space for my life work.

If you ask me, "Which is the greatest mountain on the planet?" I will always reply, "Velliangiri." I was born with an imprint of these mountains in my eyes and they have haunted me ever since. They lived within me and have been my very own navigating system, my inner radar. These mountains aren't just a matter of geography for me. They are a reservoir of all that I needed to know to create the Dhyanalinga.

The word "Velliangiri" literally means "silver mountain," and this range is so named because these mountains are covered with cloud for a large part of the year. They are also known as the "Kailash of the South" because Adiyogi, or Shiva himself, spent a little over three months upon these mountain peaks. When he came here, he was not in his usual blissful mood. (According to legend, he was angry with himself because he had failed to keep his word to one of his most ardent woman devotees.) He was intense and despondent, and that energy is still evident today; it produced a string of yogis through the tradition who were of the angry sort. They did their spiritual practice here and acquired that quality. They were not angry about anything in particular; they were simply in a certain state of intensity.

Above all, this mountain is very important for me because this is where my guru left his body. This mountain is like a temple, a living shrine, for us in this yogic tradition—a torrent of divinity, a cascade of grace.

The Way of the Mystic

There is a great curiosity in certain circles about mystical experiences. Many claim to have had extraordinary paranormal experiences which they cite as proof of their spiritual evolution.

A common word in people's spiritual lexicons nowadays is *samadhi,* which is seen as a certificate of mystical attainment.

What is samadhi?

It is a certain state of equanimity in which the intellect goes beyond its normal function of discrimination. This, in turn, loosens one from one's physical body such that there is a space between you and your body.

There are various types of samadhis, which for the sake of understanding, have been classified into eight types. Among these eight there are two broad categories: *savikalpa* (samadhis with attributes or qualities that are very pleasant, blissful, and ecstatic); and *nirvikalpa* (samadhis that are beyond pleasant and unpleasant, without attributes or qualities). In the case of nirvikalpa samadhi, there is only a single-pointed contact with the body. The rest of the energy is loose and uninvolved with the physical. These states are maintained for certain periods to help practitioners establish the distinction between themselves and their bodies.

Samadhi is a significant step in one's spiritual evolution, but it is still not the ultimate. Experiencing a certain type of samadhi does not mean you are released from the cycles of existence. It is just a new level of experience. When you were a child, you experienced life in a particular way. When you move into your adulthood, you have another level of experience. You experience the same things in a totally different way at different points in your life. Samadhis are just like this.

Some people may go into a certain level of samadhi and stay there for years because it is enjoyable. In this condition, there is no space or time and no bodily problems because the physical and psychological barriers have been broken to some extent. But this is only temporary. The moment they come out of this state, all the bodily needs and mental habits return once again.

Generally, compared to someone who is sober, someone who is slightly drunk has a different level of experience and exuberance. But everyone still has to come down at some point. All samadhis are a way of getting high without any external chemicals. If you go into these states, a new dimension does open up for you. But the crucial thing is that it does not leave you permanently transformed. You have not moved into another reality. Your level of experience has deepened, but you have not become free, in an ultimate sense.

Most enlightened beings never stayed in samadhi states. Gautama Buddha never sat and meditated for years on end after his enlightenment. Many of his disciples went into very long meditations for years. But Gautama himself never did this because he must have seen it was not necessary for him. He practiced and experienced all the eight kinds of samadhis before his enlightenment, and he discarded them. He said, "This is not it." He knew this was not going to take him to realization. Samadhi is just a heightened level of experience, a kind of inner LSD without any external input, which causes altered levels of perception. The risk is that you could get caught up with it, because it is far more beautiful than the current reality, but even the most beautiful experiences, as we know, can become a drag with time.

If you have made realization the top priority in your life, then anything that does not take you one step closer toward your ultimate freedom is meaningless. Let us say you are climbing Mount Everest: you will not take one step sideways because every iota of energy is needed to reach the peak. Now if you have to reach the peak of your consciousness, you need every iota of energy you can muster. And still it is not enough! Now, you would not want to perform any action that would distract you from the main purpose.

What is this self-realization? you might wonder. After all, all that most people are looking for is health, well-being, wealth, love, and success. Do you really need self-realization?

Let us look at this in the simplest possible way. Isn't it true that the more you know about your computer, the better you can use it? Isn't it true that your ability to use a device or instrument is directly proportional to your knowledge about it? Isn't it true that someone with a high level of dexterity and expertise can use even a simple instrument in a seemingly magical way? Have you seen some people riding on a piece of plastic they call a surfboard, doing incredible things? Just a piece of plastic, and what amazing feats of agility and grace they can perform!

Similarly, the more profound your understanding of the human mechanism is, the more magical your life will be. In every culture, there have been a few people who performed certain actions that made others believe in miracles. All these actions that are known as miracles are just born of a more profound access to life that some have enjoyed. That access, as I have said time and again, is available to everyone who cares to look deeper.

Tantra: A Technology
for Transformation

Today, there are many practices associated with the occult sciences masquerading as spiritual processes.

Let us say I am in India and you are in America. I want to send you a flower, but I am not willing to take the journey that Columbus took. If I make this flower suddenly land in your lap, this is occult. There is *nothing* spiritual about it; it is just another way of handling the physical dimension of life.

In India, we have many sophisticated occult processes. There are people who can just look at a photograph and make or break a person's life. They could ensure that the person contracts some ailment that the body could not customarily have acquired in such a short span of time. These occult practitioners can also create health, but unfortunately many of them use their ability in other ways, as there seems to be a better market for these negative talents. In any case, whether it is employed for ill health or good health is beside the point. The use of occult toward any self-oriented goal is inadvisable.

The yogic tradition is filled with stories of the great yogi Gorakhnath. Some say he lived in the eleventh century, but there are many accounts that date him much earlier. He was a disciple of Matsyendranath, an illustrious yogi in his own right. Such was his level of attainment that Matsyendranath was often venerated as a reincarnation of Shiva or Adiyogi. The lore tells us that Matsyendranath lived for about six hundred years. This need not be accepted literally or discarded as hagiography either. It essentially indicates an exceptionally long life span and the tremendous awe with which this iconic figure was regarded.

Gorakhnath became his disciple, and he adored and worshipped his master. Gorakhnath was all fire and intensity. Matsyendranath saw too much fire in him, and not enough restraint. Fire burns through many things, so Gorakhnath started burning through the walls of ignorance, and suddenly he had enormous power. Matsyendranath saw that he was running a little ahead of himself, so he told him, "Go away for fourteen years. Don't stay near me. You are imbibing too much from me."

This was the hardest thing for Gorakhnath to do. If Matsyendranath had said, "Give up your life," he would have done it at once. "Go away" was something he could not bear. But since that was what his beloved master demanded of him, he went away.

For fourteen years, he counted the days and hours, waiting for the moment when he could return. The moment the period was over, he came rushing back. When he came, he found a disciple guarding the cave where Matsyendranath lived. Gorakhnath said, "I want to see my master!"

The yogi who was guarding the cave said, "I have no such instructions, so you had better wait."

Gorakhnath flared up. He said, "I've waited for fourteen years, you fool! I don't know when *you* came here. Maybe you came here the day before yesterday. How dare you stop me!"

He pushed him aside and went into the cave. Matsyendranath was not there. Gorakhnath came back and shook the disciple and said, "Where is he? I want to see my master now!"

The disciple said, "I have no instructions to tell you where he is."

Gorakhnath could not contain himself. He used his occult powers, looked into the disciple's mind, and identified where Matsyendranath was. He then started heading in that direction. His guru was waiting for him halfway.

Matsyendranath said, "I sent you away for fourteen years, because you were beginning to become occult-oriented. You were losing sight of the spiritual process and beginning to enjoy the power that it gave you. When you come back, the first thing that you do is use occult to open up your brother disciple's mind. Another fourteen years for you."

And so he sent him away again.

There are many stories about Gorakhnath making forays into this forbidden realm, and Matsyendranath punishing him again and again. At the same time, Gorakhnath evolved finally into the greatest disciple that Matsyendranath ever produced.

This is how the practice of occult has always been treated in the yogic culture. It was never treated with respect. It was seen as a way of misusing life, of encroaching into areas where you should not. It was practiced only by certain types of people obsessed with power or money.

At the same time, occult is not always a negative thing. It has earned this reputation through misuse. Occult is essentially a technology. No science or technology is intrinsically negative. If we start using technology to kill or torture people, then after some time we think, "Enough of this damn technology!" That is what has happened to occult. Too many people misused it for personal benefit. So, generally on the spiritual path, occult is shunned.

What is often referred to as occult is broadly what we know as *tantra*. In the current understanding in society, tantra is about using very unorthodox or socially unacceptable methods. But in its classical sense, tantra simply means "technology." It has nothing to do with unbridled sexuality. It is important to make a clear distinction between the occult kind of tantra and spiritual tantra. These two were divided as "left-hand tantra" and "right-hand tantra," and are completely different in nature.

Left-hand tantra involves various rituals which may seem weirder than weird to many. The left hand is very external; you need materials and elaborate arrangements to make it happen. Occult practices, generally referred to as left-hand tantra, gave people powers to communicate across distances, to appear in two different places at the same time, and use energies to their own benefit and to the detriment of others. Right-hand tantra is more internal; it is about enabling you to use your energies to make things happen. You use all the simple aspects of life as a subjective science to turn inward and do something with yourself. The left-hand tantra is a rudimentary technology and more available to the uninitiated, while the right-hand tantra is highly refined and only available through powerful initiations.

Tantra is a certain capability; without it there is no spiritual process. If you have no tantra in you, you have no technology to transform people; all you have are words. Words can be inspirational and directional, but not transformative. A scholar cannot be labeled a guru. Without a technology for transformation there is no master. So there is no guru without tantra. Today there are too many people claiming to be gurus, but all they are doing is rehashing the scriptures. A true guru's work is to overhaul the entire human mechanism from acquired cyclical patterns of karma toward its ultimate possibility. It is like a mechanic's job, removing karmic warts! If there is no tantra or technology in him, you cannot call that person a guru.

SERPENT POWER

The word *kundalini* literally means "energy." It refers to a certain type of energy within every human being which is largely latent and unmanifest. The kundalini has always been symbolized in the yogic tradition as a coiled cobra.

A coiled cobra knows stillness of a very high quality. When the snake is motionless, it is so absolutely still that even if it is lying in your way, you will miss it. Only when it moves do you see it. But these coils hold a hidden volatile dynamism within themselves. So kundalini is referred to as a coiled cobra because this tremendous energy exists within each and every human being, but until it moves, you never realize it is there.

To live a full-fledged physical life, a minuscule amount of this physical energy is adequate. Only when the need to transcend physicality happens do you need a burst of energy which will launch you beyond this reality. It is like the difference in the quantum of energy required in air travel and in a rocket launch. Flying within the atmosphere is one thing and breaking the atmospheric barrier for space travel is quite another. Similarly, transcending physicality requires another dimension of energy altogether.

There is not a single Indian temple where there is no image of a snake. This is not because this is a culture of serpent worshippers. It signifies that a sacred space holds the possibility of arousing the unmanifest energies in you.

Snakes are known to be highly perceptive creatures. (Part of the reason for this of course is that they are stone deaf and perceive only reverberation.) The snake is particularly drawn to a person who is meditative. In the tradition, it is always said that if a yogi is meditating in a place, there will be a snake somewhere nearby. If your energies become still, the snake is naturally drawn to you.

Though physically there is a world of a difference between a snake and a human being, it is very close in terms of its energy system. If you encounter a cobra in the wild, you might find it coming into your hands without any resistance because its energies and yours are so akin to each other. Unless your chemistry shows alarm which it interprets as danger, the snake has no intention of giving up its venom, which is its wealth, the medicinal properties of which are being increasingly acknowledged in the world today.

Historically, of course, the snake has received much bad press because of the biblical story of Adam and Eve. But if you examine the tale closely, you'll see it is the snake that initiated life on this planet. Otherwise there was just a dumb couple who didn't know what to do with themselves. You and I wouldn't have been here without that wonderful serpent!

Ultimately, the rising of the kundalini energy sets the basis for a much larger perception of life. Traditional images of Adiyogi, or Shiva, depict a snake with him to indicate that his perception is at its peak. Only if energy rises to a certain level of intensity and volume can reality be perceived in its utmost purity. Otherwise every other karmic imprint that we have (which goes right back to the single-celled creature that we once were millennia ago) will interfere with the way we perceive reality.

Joy

The Beginning

Joy is a rare visitor in most people's lives. The intention of this book has been to make it your lifelong companion.

Joy is not some elusive spiritual goal. It is simply the background milieu that is needed for any aspect of your life to unfold magically and wonderfully. If joy is not the ambience of your life, even life's most pleasurable activities become burdensome. The issues of life around you can be addressed to the best of your capabilities. But once joy is your constant companion, *you* are no more an issue in your life. After that, life is a journey of endlessly unfolding celebration and discovery.

For the first time in the history of humanity, we have the necessary resources, capability, and technology to address every issue on the planet—of nourishment, health, education, you name it. We have tremendous tools of science and technology at our disposal—powerful enough to make or break the world several times over. However, if the ability to wield such powerful instruments is not accompanied by a deep sense of compassion, inclusiveness, balance, and maturity, we could be on the brink of a global disaster. Our relentless pursuit of external well-being is already on the verge of annihilating the planet.

Never before has a generation of people known the comforts and conveniences we have today. And yet, we cannot claim to be the most joyful or loving generation in history. A vast number of people live in states of constant anxiety and depression. Some are suffering their failure, but ironically, many are suffering the consequences of their success. Some are suffering their limitations, but many are suffering their freedom.

What is missing is human consciousness. Everything else is in place, but the human being is not in place. If human beings stopped obstructing the path to their own happiness, every other solution is at hand. You cannot transform the world without transforming the individual.

My life's work has been dedicated to empowering human beings to take charge of their own destinies and bringing them to a state of joyful inclusiveness so that the possibility that we are does not pass us by as a generation. Your joy, your misery, your love, your agony, your bliss, lie in *your* hands.

There is a way out. And the way out is *in*. It is only by turning inward that we can truly create a world of love, light, and laughter. This book could be a doorway to that world.

Let us make it happen.

Glossary

Adiyogi Literally, the first yogi. The being through whom the yogic sciences originated, also known as Shiva.

Agna The center of knowledge and enlightenment, agna is one of the seven major energy centers of the human body. Physically located between the eyebrows, it is also known as the "third eye."

Ahankara The sense of identity within a person, one of the consequences of which is the ego.

Akash Ether. An intermediary situation between creation and the source of creation, akash forms the subtle physical landscape on which the rest of creation unfolds.

Anahata A significant chakra, or energy center, in the human system, this is known as the "heart chakra." It is symbolized by two triangles forming a six-pointed star, where the upward-pointing triangle denotes the physical and the downward denotes the dimension beyond the physical.

Anandamayakosha Lit. bliss body. One of the sheaths, or layers, that make up the human being, according to yogic physiology. A non-physical dimension.

Ana pana sati yoga A complete system of yoga which involves bringing awareness to one's breath.

Angamardana A series of thirty-one dynamic processes to invigorate the body and reach peak physical fitness. Angamardana literally means to gain complete mastery over the limbs, organs, and other parts of the body. It revitalizes all the systems of the body, such as the muscular, skeletal, nervous, circulatory, and respiratory systems.

Annamayakosha The physical sheath, or layer, in yogic physiology, this is also referred to as the food body, since the physical body is essentially constituted of the food that one consumes.

Asana, Yogasana Yoga means union or to merge, while asana means a physical posture. Those postures that allow one to achieve union with one's higher nature are referred to as yogasanas. One of the eight limbs of yoga.

Avadhuta One who has risen above duality. Generally describes a yogi or saint who is in a constant state of inner bliss.

Ayurveda, Ayurvedic Lit. the science of life. An ancient Indian system of food and medicine, which employs herbs and earth elements to correct systemic irregularities, and promote health and well-being.

Bhakti yoga Lit. yoga of devotion. Refers to the spiritual path of self-realization through love and devotion. Characterized by an intense desire for union with the object of one's devotion. One of the four paths of yoga.

Bhuta shuddhi The most fundamental practice in yoga, bhuta shuddhi means the cleansing of the five elements within the human system.

Bhuta siddhi A state where one has gained mastery over the five elements within the human system; a level of expertise that promotes well-being and the ability to access dimensions beyond the physical.

Brahmarandra *Brahma* means the ultimate and *randra* means opening or cavity. Another name for the sahasrara chakra, which is located at the fontanel, or the soft spot at the top of an infant's head.

Buddhi Faculty of discrimination, analysis, logical and rational thought; the intellect.

Chakra Lit. wheel. Also refers to the junctions of nadis (channels) in the energy body. Though seven major chakras are associated with the human body, there are a total of 114 chakras, two of which are outside the human body.

Chidakash, or **Chidakasha** The etheric dimension of intelligence.

Chitta Pure intelligence, unsullied by memory. The deepest, most fundamental dimension of the human mind; a person in touch with this dimension is said to have access to the source of creation.

Chit shakti Lit. the power of the mind. Also a meditation designed by Sadhguru to enhance the power of the mind.

Dharana A yogic process in which the subject maintains an unwavering focus on an object and establishes experiential contact with it. One of the eight limbs of yoga.

Dhyana, or **Dhyan** A yogic process of maintaining focus in which either the subject or object is absorbed into the other. One of the eight limbs of yoga.

Dhyanalinga A powerful energy form at Isha Yoga Center in India, it was consecrated by Sadhguru exclusively for the purpose of meditation.

Gnana, Gnana yoga Attainment of a state where one's intelligence is employed to reach one's ultimate nature. One of the four paths of yoga.

Guru Lit. dispeller of darkness. A spiritual master, a realized being who guides spiritual seekers toward liberation.

Hatha yoga A form of yoga involving physical postures and practices. Used as both a purificatory and preparatory step for meditation and higher dimensions of spiritual experience.

Ida One of the three major pranic channels in the human body. Located on the left side of the body, it is feminine and intuitive in nature.

Kalpavriksha Lit. a wishing tree. In yoga, a well-established mind is referred to as a kalpavriksha.

Karma Lit. action. Used to refer to the composite expression of past actions, which binds one to the body and determines many aspects about a person.

Karma yoga Yoga of action. The science of performing actions that liberate rather than entangle a human being. One of the four paths of yoga.

Kriya, Kriya yoga Lit. internal action. Transforming one's inner energies to reach one's ultimate nature. One of the four paths of yoga.

Kundalini Fundamental life energy, which rises upward through the practice of yoga. Depicted as a snake coiled at the base of the spine.

Linga Lit. the first or primordial form. A perfect ellipsoid, it is the fundamental form in the cosmic geometry.

Mahasamadhi Highest form of equanimity that entails the complete dissolution or neutralization of the personal in the universal, whereby all traits of individual nature are transcended. Also known as Nirvana, and Mahaparinibbana in other Eastern spiritual traditions.

Manas A dimension of the mind, distinct from the intellect, which is a complex amalgam of memory, and molds thoughts and emotions.

Mandala Refers to the physiognomic cycle, a time period of forty to forty-eight days, which is the natural period of many physiological processes in the body.

Manipuraka The chakra, or energy center, located a little below the navel. It is associated with the vital energy needed for survival and active engagement in the outside world.

Manomayakosha The mental body. One of the five sheaths of the yogic physiology.

Muladhara Located at the perineum, the muladhara is the foundation of the energy body.

Nadi The channels through which the life force, or prana, flows in the energy body.

Namaskar The traditional Indian practice of putting two hands together, which harmonizes the two dimensions (right-left, masculine-feminine, etc.) within a person, and promotes an experience of unity and sovereignty within the self, while acknowledging the same in others.

Nirvikalpa Lit. without qualities. A type of samadhi, or equanimity, beyond all qualities or attributes, where a person's contact with their body is minimal.

Pingala One of the major energy channels of the body. Located on the right side of the body, the pingala is considered masculine in nature.

Prana Fundamental life force; vital energy.

Pranamayakosha The energy body. One of the five sheaths of yogic physiology.

Pratishtha Process of consecration or energizing an object or space. These processes are mainly of two kinds: mantra pratishtha, through chanting appropriate mantras and performing rituals; and prana pratishtha, through a direct process involving the consecrator's own prana-shakti, or life energies.

Sadhana Lit. tool or device. Spiritual practices which are used as a means to self-realization.

Sahasrara The chakra, or energy center, of the human system located at the fontanel or crown of the head.

Samadhi Deep state of equanimity, one of the eight limbs of yoga. Greatly celebrated in the Indian spiritual tradition, the experience of samadhi is therapeutic and deeply transformative in nature.

Samsara The repetitive and cyclical nature of the physical world and the domain of karma, which offers the necessary stability for the making of life.

Samyukti The state of having a well-established mind, which does not work against itself.

Savikalpa Lit. with qualities. Used to refer to types of samadhi, or equanimity, with qualities or attributes.

Shavasana Lit. corpse posture. One of the eighty-four asanas in the classical yogic tradition. Practiced for its capacity to promote restfulness and for its rejuvenating impact on the system.

Shi-va, Shiva Lit. that which is not. Used to refer to limitless space; also refers to Adiyogi, the first yogi, who experienced a state of union with this limitless space.

Sushumna The central channel in the energy body which conducts kundalini, or the life force.

Surya kriya A powerful process of activating the sun within. *Surya* means sun, and *kriya* means an inner energy process. Designed as a holistic process for health, wellness, and inner well-being, surya kriya is also a complete spiritual process.

Surya namaskar An ancient yogic practice, which is not only a way of balancing the system, but also a way of becoming receptive to the sun, based on the logic that all life is solar-powered.

Surya shakti A yogic practice which stimulates the sun within the human system.

Swadhishthana Lit. abode of the self; the chakra or energy center situated just above the genitals.

Tamas Inertia. Refers to one of the three qualities of existence; the other two are rajas, or dynamism, and sattva, or equanimity.

Tantra Lit. technology. The technology of spiritual transformation.

Vasanas Tendencies or inclinations; subliminal traits in a human being, the residue of desires and actions.

Vedanta Lit. end of perceivable knowledge. The philosophy or the teachings of the Upanishads, the speculative and metaphysical commentaries on the Vedas.

Vignanamayakosha One of the five layers of the body, which is known as a transitory body. It facilitates the transition from the physical to the non-physical.

Vishesh Gnana Extraordinary knowing or knowing beyond sense perception.

Vishuddhi One of the seven major chakras, vishuddhi is the center of power and vision. It is located at the pit of the throat.

Yantra Lit. form. An energy form, which can be designed and consecrated in different ways to bring prosperity and well-being to one's life.

Yoga Lit. to yoke or unite. A state of being where the individual experiences a state of union with existence. Also refers to the ancient spiritual science, which gives methods and technologies to reach that state.

Yogi One who has known the union of existence. A person who is in a state of yoga.

INNER ENGINEERING

Inner Engineering is an opportunity to engineer an inner transformation and deepen your perception, bringing about a dimensional shift in the very way you look at your life, work and the world.

It is offered as an intensive program for personal growth and establishes the possibility of exploring higher dimensions of life, in addition to optimizing health and success.

Inner Engineering provides tools and solutions that empower and enable you to create your life the way you want it. It is a doorway to explore the basics of life, using time-tested methods from the yogic sciences.

The course imparts practical wisdom to manage your body, mind, emotions, and the fundamental life energy within. Inner Engineering includes the powerful Shambhavi Mahamudra Kriya—a yogic practice of immense transformative power and antiquity—which can bring your whole system into alignment and harmony, thus enabling you to uncover your full potential.

ISHA FOUNDATION

Isha Foundation is a non-religious, not-for-profit, public service organization founded by Sadhguru, which addresses all aspects of human well-being. Isha is essentially a volunteer-based organization with over 3 million full-time and part-time volunteers in 300 centers worldwide. It is headquartered at the Isha Yoga Center located at the Velliangiri foothills in Tamil

Nadu, and at the Isha Institute of Inner-sciences in Tennessee, United States.

From its powerful yoga programs for inner transformation to its inspiring projects for society and environment, Isha's activities are designed to create an inclusive culture that is the basis for global harmony and progress. This approach has gained worldwide recognition and reflects in Isha Foundation's special consultative status with the Economic and Social Council (ECOSOC) of the United Nations.

Project GreenHands (PGH) is Isha's public reforestation effort aimed at inspiring the population of India to reverse environmental degradation and promote sustainable living. PGH has facilitated the planting of 30 million trees thus far. It set a Guinness Record for most number of saplings planted in a day—852,587—in 2006. The Indian Government has recognized Project GreenHands' positive ecological impact by awarding PGH the Indira Gandhi Paryavaran Puraskar—India's highest environmental award.

Action for Rural Rejuvenation (ARR) is Isha's rural revitalization program offering holistic healthcare, community rehabilitation and life-skills training in over 4600 villages, serving a population of 7 million people in rural India. ARR is not just about giving economic or administrative help, but rather seeks to empower rural people to transform their life.

Isha Vidhya is a pioneering initiative committed to raising the level of education and literacy among rural children. It seeks to create equal opportunities for all to participate in and benefit from India's economic growth. Isha Vidhya is currently involved with over 79,000 students and 520 schools, to open the door for rural children to successfully pursue higher studies and gainful employment. Isha has also partnered with various state governments to offer simple yogic practices throughout the year, to 30 million students in 25,000 schools across India.

ABOUT THE TYPE

This book was set in Sabon, a typeface designed by the well-known German typographer Jan Tschichold (1902–74). Sabon's design is based upon the original letter forms of sixteenth-century French type designer Claude Garamond and was created specifically to be used for three sources: foundry type for hand composition, Linotype, and Monotype. Tschichold named his typeface for the famous Frankfurt typefounder Jacques Sabon (c. 1520–80).